JUDICIAL REVIEW

in the

CONTEMPORARY WORLD

JUDICIAL REVIEW

in the

CONTEMPORARY WORLD

by MAURO CAPPELLETTI

Professor of Law, Stanford University
Professor of Law and Director,
Institute of Comparative Law,
University of Florence (Italy)

THE BOBBS-MERRILL COMPANY, INC.
A SUBSIDIARY OF HOWARD W. SAMS & CO., INC.
PUBLISHERS • Indianapolis • Kansas City • New York

In the realm of thought, it is supremely just and right that all frontiers should be swept away.

There is too little of high spiritual value scattered over the earth for any epoch to say: we are utterly self-sufficient; or even: we prefer our own.

JACOB BURCKHARDT

PREFACE

Few institutions reveal the temper of our times as clearly as judicial review of the constitutionality of legislation. This comparative analysis of judicial review[1] attempts to demonstrate not only that the institution represents a fascinating synthesis of two seemingly contradictory schools of thought, but also that it tells us much of our own psychological responses to the tyrannies of our age.

Written constitutions, and the subordination by the courts of statutory law to those constitutions, represent innovations with deep philosophical roots. From the earliest times men have sought to create or discover a hierarchy of laws and to guarantee this hierarchy.[2] Indeed, this search is one aspect of man's never-ending attempt to find something immutable in the continuous change which is his destiny. Laws change, but the Law must remain, and with it the fundamental values; a law which contravenes that Higher Law is not a law at all.

Basically this doctrine lies at the root of all natural law theories, whether secular or divine, and implies the right to disobey the unjust law, whatever sacrifice disobedience may entail. Of course, from a realistic point of view, these theories themselves are based on an illusion. The Law also changes, and even the fundamental values are mutable. One could say, to paraphrase Benjamin Constant, that the liberty of today is not that of other times, and the same can be said of justice and all other values. But the utopian desire which natural law doctrines express is an irrepressible facet of human nature, and thus natural law theories will be continually revived, especially in moments of acute crisis.

One such revival has occurred in our own time. Particularly in the civil law world, the 19th century was heavily influenced by positivist thought, which feared any attempt by the judiciary to impose "higher" or "constitutional" standards on ordinary legisla-

---

[1] This study is primarily meant for students. It is an expanded version of a series of lectures given in 1965 at the National University of Mexico and of later seminars conducted at various universities in Italy, France, Austria, and the United States.

The lectures have been translated into Spanish by C. Gómez Lara and H. Fix Zamudio; M. CAPPELLETTI, EL CONTROL JUDICIAL DE LA CONSTITUCIONALIDAD DE LAS LEYES EN EL DERECHO COMPARADO (Publicaciones de le Revista de la Facultad de Derecho de México, 1966). For the original Italian text see IL CONTROLLO GIUDIZIARIO DI COSTITUZIONALITÀ DELLE LEGGI NEL DIRITTO COMPARATO (Milano, Giuffrè, 1968, reprinted 1970).

[2] For historical precedents see Ch. II *infra*.

tion. The popular legislature was seen as the only source of law, and its statutes were to control all cases brought before the courts. When the Nazi-Fascist era shook this faith in the legislature, people began to reconsider the judiciary as a check against legislative disregard of principles once considered immutable. They began, in a sense, to "positivize" these principles, to put them in written form and to provide legal barriers against their violation.

This process took place in three stages. The first step was the written constitution, primarily conceived as a codification of individual and social values. Here we find the necessarily vague terms of these values being transformed into positive law, in an attempt to give legal significance and positive meaning to meta-legal ideals.

The second step was to give a "rigid" character to modern constitutions, conferring a relative immutability on the superior law and the values it enshrines. This rigidity was in marked contrast to such nineteenth century constitutions as Italy's *Statuto Albertino* which the legislature could change at any time by an ordinary statute.

The final step was to provide a means for guaranteeing the constitution, separate from the legislative power itself[3] and embodied in the active work of the judges or, in some systems, of a special Constitutional Court. This active work of the judiciary makes the vague terms of constitutional provisions concrete and gives them practical application. Through this work the static terms of the constitution become alive, adapting themselves to the conditions of everyday life, and the values contained in the "Higher Law" become really effective. Hence, the framework of modern constitutions and judicial review synthesize the ineffective and abstract ideals of natural law with the concrete provisions of positive law. Through modern constitutionalism, in short, natural law, put on an historical and realistic footing, has found a new place in legal thought.

Another characteristic of modern constitutionalism, beyond the desire to incorporate immutable ideals into positive law, shows a similar convergence of natural law and positivism. Natural law proclaimed its ideals not only immutable, but also universally valid, while positivism confined the validity of law to the boundaries of national sovereignty. In modern constitutionalism there is a clear trend toward a universal acceptance of certain values. Thus, though

---

[3] For attempts to establish legislative and other nonjudicial controls see Ch. I, §§ 1-5 *infra*.

the constitution remains the supreme law for a particular state, we may find remarkable and growing similarity in the ideals of many, particularly Western, constitutions.

This trend is especially apparent in the context of judicial review. Subsequent chapters describe the spread of judicial review from the United States to numerous other countries, in Europe and elsewhere. With its recent introduction in Yugoslavia it has even taken root in an entirely different ideological and constitutional environment. Moreover, it will be seen that originally there were two entirely distinct systems of judicial review, separated by deep theoretical differences. But, even here, the converging trend of modern jurisprudence is reflected in a muting of the original sharp contrast. It is precisely in this blurring of sharp ideological distinctions, and in this gradual tendency towards harmonization of legal institutions, that the comparative method reveals its importance.

We live in an age characterized above all by cultural and economic movements cutting across national boundaries. This internationalism is reflected in the enormous growth of interest in comparative law, not only in the constitutional area, but in every branch of jurisprudence. Traditional natural law theories were doomed to failure because they could not give substance to their airy formulations and had no instrument to put them into effect. Positivism, on the other hand, limited to the actual application of the law on a purely national level, could not satisfy the grander desires of man. The modern comparative school seeks to combine the virtues of both natural law and positivism by adopting the realistic methods of positivism in the search for common elements in legal institutions of various nations and the common values expressed in them.[4] The comparative method is the indispensable tool

---

[4] In the field of private international law, others have already used the comparative method to begin a genuine "third school," the forerunner of which was Ernst Rabel. This school synthesized both the universalist school of the 19th century, headed by such people as Savigny and Mancini, and the positivist and particularist school prevalent in Europe at the turn of the century with the emergence of such scholars as Bartin, Kahn, Dicey, and Anzilotti. See K. Zweigert, *Die dritte Schule im internationalen Privatrecht. Zur neueren Wissenschaftsgeschichte des Kollisionsrechts*, in FESTSCHRIFT FÜR LEO RAAPE 35 ff. (Hamburg, Rechts- und Staatswissenschaftlicher Verlag, 1948). *See also* M. CAPPELLETTI, PROCESSO E IDEOLOGIE 339 ff., 368 ff., 382 ff. (Bologna, Il Mulino, 1969); and M. CAPPELLETTI, EL VALOR DE LAS SENTENCIAS Y DE LAS NORMAS EXTRANJERAS EN EL PROCESO CIVIL 5 ff., 57 ff., 85 ff. (Buenos Aires, Ediciones Jurídicas Europa-América, 1968). This development, however, is not confined to private international law, but can be found in constitutional law, and the law in general. I would consider it to be the central feature of modern jurisprudence.

of this new approach, for it offers the practical means by which the search for the "common core" of legal systems can be pursued.[5]

Constitutions express the "positivization" of higher values; *judicial review* is the method for rendering these values effective; and the *comparative method* is the instrument of the movement towards harmonization and of the search for internationally acceptable values. These three are essentially linked together and form an integral part of the new direction in modern jurisprudence.

[5] *See* R.B. Schlesinger, *The Common Core of Legal Systems: An Emerging Subject of Comparative Study,* in XXth Century Comparative and Conflicts Law. Legal Essays in Honor of Hessel E. Yntema 65 ff. (Leyden, Sythoff, 1961).

ACKNOWLEDGMENTS

This book has been made possible by a grant from the Italian National Research Council and by the Fondazione G. Agnelli of Turin.

At the outset, I should like to thank Mr. David Wilson and Mr. Robert G. Werner, graduates of the Law School of the University of California at Berkeley, and Mr. James R. Gordley, a student at the Harvard Law School, for their invaluable assistance in revising the style and content of the English version of this study. I should also like to thank Mr. Robert Englehart, a law graduate from Oxford University, and Mr. Thomas R. Toothaker, a student in the School of Law of Stanford University, for their help in bringing this book to its fruition. My deep appreciation also goes to Dr. Vera Bolgár, the Executive Secretary of the American Journal of Comparative Law, for her generous help in the preparation of the Index.

Among the many who kindly read the manuscript and gave me the benefit of their criticism and suggestions, I wish to mention particularly Professors John C. Adams of Syracuse University, Guido Calabresi of Yale, Louis L. Jaffe of Harvard, Gerald Gunther and John H. Merryman of Stanford, Stefan A. Riesenfeld of Berkeley, and Yasuhei Taniguchi of Kyoto University, as well as all my students at the Law Schools of Stanford and Harvard in 1968 and 1969.

TABLE OF CONTENTS

CHAPTER I

JUDICIAL AND POLITICAL CONTROLS OF CONSTITUTIONALITY

§ 1. Political control of constitutionality: general

Judicial review of the constitutionality of legislation presents an exciting and perplexing encounter between legislator and judge, between statute and judgment. However, judicial review is but a part of a much larger whole. If one defines "constitutional justice" as that condition in which citizens may trust their government to uphold certain rights considered inviolable, it is clear that judicial review of statutes is only one way of attaining this happy state. In fact, in a given country political factors may perhaps provide a better check than the courts on attempts to establish majoritarian tyranny. Even when speaking of strictly judicial protection of constitutionality (the *Verfassungsgerichtsbarkeit* of the Germans), one must grant that formal review of statutes for conformity with a written document is only one of the judicial means available for this end.[1] This chapter will attempt to fit judicial review into this larger picture, showing the wide range of means, political and judicial, available to a country wishing to restrain the arbitrary exercise of governmental power. Later chapters will analyze judicial review: its history, the forms it has taken, and the trends in its evolution.

In certain countries a *political* review operates alongside or instead of *judicial* review. Usually under these systems the control

---

[1] On the various facets of constitutional justice see, for instance, R. MARCIC, VERFASSUNG UND VERFASSUNGSGERICHT 93-112 (Wien, Springer Verlag, 1963); Geck, *Judicial Review of Statutes: A Comparative Survey of Present Institutions and Practices,* 51 CORNELL L.Q. 250, 252 (1966). Two of the most important aspects of *Verfassungsgerichtsbarkeit,* aside from review of statutes, are, (1) resolution of jurisdictional disputes between various state organs, and (2) criminal trials of high state officials accused of serious violations of the constitution. Both the Italian and German Constitutions confer jurisdiction over such questions on the special constitutional courts of those countries. Arts. 61, 93(1), 98(2) of the German Basic Law, and art. 134 of the Italian Constitution.

is not exercised after the enactment of the law, but is *preventive;* it intervenes before the law comes into force. Sometimes the control is merely consultative, in that an opinion is given which does not have binding force upon the legislature and the executive.

Some of these political controls are indirect; without formally declaring statutes unconstitutional, they make it difficult for the legislature to change the accepted constitutional order. The American system of "checks and balances" does this by requiring that radical changes in the political order have the assent of nearly all major political groups in the country. Similarly, many would say that the combination of single member districts and strict party discipline in Great Britain has made it very difficult for minority groups intent upon extreme change to attain power.[2]

Other political controls are more explicit: elected representatives, or their appointees, are authorized to consider the conformity of proposed legislation with a written constitution. In the past, these bodies enjoyed only theoretical powers to annul legislation. Thus neither the *Supremo Poder Conservador* included in the Mexican Constitution of 1836, nor its model, the *Sénat Conservateur* of the French Constitution of the Year VIII (1799), was able to exercise its sweeping powers, though both served as precedents for twentieth century attempts at nonjudicial control of constitutionality.[3] Three of these attempts will now be examined.

§ 2.   Political control of constitutionality: France

France certainly offers the most typical and numerous examples

---

[2] PATTERNS OF GOVERNMENT 175-77 (S. Beer, A. Ulam, *et al.* (eds.), New York, Random House, 1962).

There were examples of preventive and consultative controls within the United States. The Council of Revision of early New York had veto power over all bills before they became law; it consisted of the governor, chancellor, and judges of the highest court. A merely consultative control was exercised by the Pennsylvania Council of Errors; the Council would advise the legislature to repeal whatever laws it deemed contrary to the Constitution. C.G. HAINES, THE AMERICAN DOCTRINE OF JUDICIAL SUPREMACY 73-87 (Berkeley, University of California Press, 2d ed. 1932).

[3] *See* H. FIX ZAMUDIO, EL JUICIO DE AMPARO 215 (México, Porrúa, 1964); I. BURGOA, EL JUICIO DE AMPARO 98 ff. (México, Porrúa, 6th ed. 1968). On the *Sénat conservateur* of the French Constitution of the Year VIII see, for instance, H. ESMEIN, 1 ELÉMENTS DE DROIT CONSTITUTIONNEL FRANÇAIS ET COMPARÉ 602, 614, 638 (Paris, Sirey, 8th ed. 1927); 2 *id.* 77 f. (Paris, Sirey, 1928); J. ELLUL, 2(2) HISTOIRE DES INSTITUTIONS 693 (Paris, Presses Universitaires de France, 1956); M. DUVERGER, DROIT PUBLIC 23 f. (Paris, Presses Universitaires de France, 3d ed. 1963); G. BURDEAU, DROIT CONSTITUTIONNEL ET INSTITUTIONS POLITIQUES 95 f. (Paris, Pichon et Durand-Auzias, 14th ed. 1969).

of political, as opposed to judicial, control.[4] In fact, French constitutions have always denied the power of judicial review for historical and ideological reasons.[5] This seems to be true even of the present French Constitution of 1958. This Constitution does not grant the judges a general power to review the constitutionality of legislation.[6] On the other hand, provision is made for a *Conseil Constitutionnel* which was established by the subsequently modified "ordonnance" of 7th November 1958. It is composed of all ex-presidents of the Republic and nine more members, three of whom are nominated by the President of the Republic, three by the President of the *Assemblée Nationale*, and three by the President of the *Sénat*. In addition to other functions which are not of immediate interest, such as review of the proper conduct of presidential and parliamentary elections,[7] the *Conseil Constitutionnel* has a function which French lawyers call "le contrôle de la constitutionnalité des lois."

This "control" is exercised in the following way. When a legislative enactment or an international treaty has been drafted but not yet promulgated, the President of the Republic, the Prime Minister, or the President of one of the Houses of Parliament (the *Assemblée Nationale* and the *Sénat*) can refer the bill or treaty to the *Conseil Constitutionnel* for a decision on its conformity with the Constitu-

---

[4] On the countries which do not have judicial review of the constitutionality of legislation see generally Battaglini, *Contributo allo studio comparato del controllo di costituzionalità*, 12 Rivista trimestrale di diritto pubblico 663-770 (1962).

[5] See Ch. 2, § 4 *infra*. French *doctrine* is, however, not lacking in several authoritative opinions in favor of this control. References in Jeanne Lemasurier, La constitution de 1946 et le contrôle juridictionnel du législateur 163 (Paris, Pichon et Durand-Auzias, 1954) (Hauriou, Duguit, Jèze, Barthélemy); Dietze, *Judicial Review in Europe*, 55 Mich. L. Rev. 539, 541 ff. (1957). See also H. Galland, Le contrôle judiciaire de la constitutionnalité des lois aux Etats-Unis 18 f. (Paris, Sirey, 1932). The contrary view, which holds good for current French theory, can be seen, *e.g.*, in G. Burdeau, Les libertés publiques 71-74 (Paris, Pichon et Durand-Auzias, 3d ed. 1966).

[6] *But see* the bold thesis of M. Duverger, Institutions politiques et droit constitutionnel 663-65 (Paris, Presses Universitaires de France, 10th ed. 1968). This thesis has not been accepted by French courts and writers. See also the references in Francine Batailler, Le Conseil d'Etat juge constitutionnel 17 (Paris, Pichon et Durand-Auzias, 1966); C.-A. Colliard, Libertés publiques 139 f. (Paris, Dalloz, 1968); Buerstedde, *Kontrolle der rechtsetzenden Gewalt durch Conseil constitutionnel und Conseil d'État nach der französischen Verfassung vom 4. Oktober 1958*, 12 Jahrbuch des öffentlichen Rechts der Gegenwart 163 f. (1963); Engel, *Judicial Review and Political Preview of Legislation in Post-War France*, 6 Inter-Am. L. Rev. 53, 63-65, 68-72 (1964).

[7] *See generally* Waline, *The Constitutional Council of the French Republic*, 12 Am. J. Comp. L. 483 ff. (1963).

tion. For the "organic" laws *(lois organiques)*—which on the whole are those concerned with the organization of public bodies—referral to the *Conseil Constitutionnel* is compulsory. The *Conseil* must give its decisions within one month or, in certain cases, within eight days; in the interim period the promulgation of the law is suspended. Decisions of the *Conseil Constitutionnel* are issued on a majority vote after a proceeding conducted in secret. There are no oral hearings, no adversary litigation, no genuine parties to a case. Written briefs from the interested public bodies, however, are admitted.[8] If the *Conseil* finds the proposed law unconstitutional, it cannot be promulgated without amendment to the Constitution.

French commentators generally recognize that the function of the *Conseil Constitutionnel* is not judicial,[9] as indicated by its assigned role under the Constitution of 1958 and its subsequent behavior. First, the *Conseil* may not convene on the initiative of private parties; rather, the right to convene the *Conseil* is reserved to a few political figures who will usually belong to the same

---

[8] *See generally id.* at 487 f., 492 f.; Buerstedde, *supra* note 6, at 169 f.; Eisenmann & Hamon, *La Juridiction Constitutionnelle en Droit Français (1875-1961),* in MAX-PLANCK-INSTITUT FÜR AUSLÄNDISCHES ÖFFENTLICHES RECHT UND VÖLKERRECHT, VERFASSUNGSGERICHTSBARKEIT IN DER GEGENWART. LÄNDERBERICHTE UND RECHTSVERGLEICHUNG 264 ff., 279 f. (H. Mosler (ed.), Köln-Berlin, Heymanns, 1962); Favoreu, *Le Conseil Constitutionnel régulateur de l'activité normative des pouvoirs publics,* 83 REVUE DU DROIT PUBLIC ET DE LA SCIENCE POLITIQUE EN FRANCE ET À L'ÉTRANGER 100 ff., 103 ff. (1967).

[9] "It would be highly misleading to characterize the functions of the Constitutional Council as judicial review." H.J. ABRAHAM, THE JUDICIAL PROCESS 298 (Oxford University Press, 2d ed. 1968). A similar judgment is made by J. BROSSARD, LA COUR SUPRÊME ET LA CONSTITUTION. LE FORUM CONSTITUTIONNEL AU CANADA 44 (Presses de l'Université de Montréal, 1968); BURDEAU, *supra* note 3, at 96, 109; C.J. FRIEDRICH, THE IMPACT OF AMERICAN CONSTITUTIONALISM ABROAD 89 (Boston University Press, 1967); E. VESCOVI, EL PROCESO DE INCONSTITUCIONALIDAD DE LA LEY 58 f., 71 (Montevideo, Facultad de Derecho y Ciencias Sociales, 1967); Cole, *Three Constitutional Courts: A Comparison,* 53 AM. POL. SCI. REV. 963, 968 n.17 (1959); Engelhardt, *Das richterliche Prüfungsrecht im modernen Verfassungsstaat,* 8 JAHRBUCH DES ÖFFENTLICHEN RECHTS DER GEGENWART 121 (1959). *See also* BATAILLER, *supra* note 6, at 33, 34, 37 f.; COLLIARD, *supra* note 6, at 35 f., 127; Colliard, *Les libertés publiques en France,* in TRAVAUX ET RECHERCHES DE L'INSTITUT DE DROIT COMPARÉ DE L'UNIVERSITÉ DE PARIS, VIIe CONGRÈS INTERNATIONAL DE DROIT COMPARÉ—UPPSALA, 1966. CONTRIBUTIONS FRANÇAISES: ETUDES DE DROIT CONTEMPORAIN 438 (Paris, Editions Cujas, 1966); Ehrmann, *Die Verfassungsentwicklung im Frankreich der Fünften Republik,* 10 JAHRBUCH DES ÖFFENTLICHEN RECHTS DER GEGENWART 375 (1961); Eisenmann & Hamon, *supra* note 8, at 256 f.; further references in Buerstedde, *supra* note 6, at 149 f. Unconvincing are the opposite opinions of Favoreu, *supra* note 8, at 115 ff. and of Massart, *Il controllo di legittimità costituzionale nella nuova Costituzione francese,* in 2 STUDI IN MEMORIA DI L. MOSSA 603, 612 f. (Padova, Cedam, 1961).

majority which passed the challenged statute.[10] Second, the control is exercisable only prior to promulgation of the statute, and is therefore merely preventive;[11] it is no more than one stage in the whole legislative process.[12] Finally, the *Conseil Constitutionnel* itself has further circumscribed its already limited jurisdiction. For example, the *Conseil* has refused to examine issues not raised by the

---

[10] On the political nature of the *Conseil* in regard to its members, proceedings, etc., see Buerstedde, *supra* note 6, at 149 f. *See also* Eisenmann & Hamon, *supra* note 8, at 286. *But see* Favoreu, *supra* note 8, at 66 ff., 86 f.

The officials who may convene the *Conseil Constitutionnel* are the President of the Republic, the Premier, or the President of one or the other Assembly (art. 61 of the Constitution of 1958). Their limited number and the complete lack of party initiative have led to the comment that ". . . si le Parlement et le Gouvernement (y compris le President de la République) s'entendent pour violer la Constitution, le Conseil Constitutionnel est impuissant." BATAILLER, *supra* note 6, at 35.

[11] On this point see, *e.g.*, F. Pierandrei, under *Corte costituzionale*, in 10 ENCICLOPEDIA DEL DIRITTO 887 f. *sub b* (Milano, Giuffrè, 1962).

In fact, as has been observed elsewhere (Cappelletti & Adams, *Judicial Review of Legislation: European Antecedents and Adaptations,* 79 HARV. L. REV. 1207, 1212 f. (1966)), the functions of the *Conseil Constitutionnel* as regards control of Parliamentary legislation resemble much less a real judicial review of legislation than "the practice of submitting bills to the *Conseil d'État* before they are presented to the Parliament." This practice, traditional in France, has its counterpart in Italy (G. ZANOBINI, 3 CORSO DI DIRITTO AMMINISTRATIVO 46 (Milano, Giuffrè, 6th ed. 1958)), as well as in Holland and Belgium (P. WIGNY, 1 DROIT CONSTITUTIONNEL 189 ff. (Bruxelles, Bruylant, 1952)). Clearly, however, it does not represent one of the judicial functions of the Council of State.

[12] *Cf.* Engelhardt, *supra* note 9, at 121 (the *Conseil Constitutionnel* portrayed "als ein Glied des Gesetzgebungsapparats").

I would consider of minor importance the discussion of whether the *Conseil Constitutionnel* exercises an "activité juridique," as affirmed by Favoreu, *supra* note 8, at 5 ff., esp. at 14 ff., 40 ff., 64 ff., or rather an "activité politique," as others view it. It may be admitted that the "binding opinion" of the *Conseil* is a legal opinion and not solely an evaluation of the political merits. But that does not mean it is a genuine *judicial* judgment. It is much more important to take a look at the overall picture. An objective view reveals in France a type of control over constitutionality which is fairly limited and, in a comparative light, decidedly rudimentary. This is not so much from the point of view of the "legal" guarantees (independence, impartiality) of the organ exercising the control, but rather because of the following limitations: (1) as to *subjects,* there are only four officials with the right to seek review; (2) as to *objects,* there is no control by the *Conseil Constitutionnel* over executive decrees having the force of law, which have, under the Fifth Republic, been assuming a very extensive role covering, for example, the entire field of civil procedure. *See* H. SOLUS & R. PERROT, 1 DROIT JUDICIAIRE PRIVÉ § 78 (Paris, Sirey, 1961); (3) as to the *time* when the mechanism of review may be put into operation, all review becomes impossible once the law has been promulgated. Clearly this is a system which neglects the fact that both ordinary laws and constitutions are subject to evolution and that it is impossible to foresee at the outset—before the promulgation—every possible meaning of a law, and hence every possible aspect of unconstitutionality. *Cf.* Geck, *supra* note 1, at 272. The limitations and slight practical importance of the French system of review have been revealed, for that matter, by the extremely small number of cases in which the constitutional function of the *Conseil Constitutionnel* has been exercised. See the statistics up to December 1966 given by Favoreu, *supra* note 8, at 89, 118 n.302.

convening authority,[13] and it has not asked if statutes violated individual rights guaranteed by the Constitution or by the Declaration of the Rights of Man.[14] The *Conseil*, it seems, has barred the way to its own evolution as a *judicial* entity. Its function—to prevent legislative encroachment upon the executive jurisdiction—is, and apparently will remain, political.

§ 3.   Political control of constitutionality: Italy

Italy furnishes a typical example of political control of legislation in a country where judicial review also exists.[15] This political control rests with the President of the Republic. He has the duty of promulgating laws approved by Parliament, but he has discretion to suspend promulgation and ask the two Houses to subject the bill to further consideration. Under the Constitution (art. 74, para. 2), if the two Houses again approve the bill, the President is required to promulgate it. Some, however, interpret this provision restrictively.[16] The primary duty of the President of the Republic under the Constitution (arts. 90 and 91) is to guarantee the observance of the Constitution. It is claimed therefore that, if the President considers a bill unconstitutional which has been reapproved by Parliament, he must refuse to promulgate it.[17] Here we see the possibility of a conflict of competence between state authorities—in this example, between the President of the Republic

---

[13] *E.g.*, decision of 20 January 1961, in 1962 RECUEIL DALLOZ (JURISPRUDENCE) 177, with note by L. Hamon.

[14] *E.g.*, decision of 15 January 1960, in 1960 RECUEIL DALLOZ (JURISPRUDENCE) 293. BATAILLER, *supra* note 6, at 38 f.; Geck, *supra* note 1, at 271.

[15] The Italian Constitution, to be exact, provides for at least two types of political control. Apart from that mentioned in the text, there is that exercised by the central government over regional legislation under art. 127, paras. 1-3, of the Constitution. *See, e.g.*, Esposito, *Il controllo giurisdizionale sulla costituzionalità delle leggi in Italia*, 5 (pt. 1) RIVISTA DI DIRITTO PROCESSUALE 294 f. (1950).

[16] *See, e.g.*, Calamandrei, *Corte costituzionale e autorità giudiziaria*, 11 (pt. 1) RIVISTA DI DIRITTO PROCESSUALE 18 f. (1956).

[17] On the analogous "Gesetzesprüfungskompetenz" of the *Bundespräsident* in the Federal Republic of Germany see the references in Hall, *Überlegungen zur Prüfungskompetenz des Bundespräsidenten*, 20 JURISTENZEITUNG 305 ff., esp. 306 f. (1965). The Federal President in more than one case has asserted the power to refuse his signature to legislation he considers unconstitutional, though this power is not specifically granted him by the Constitution. *See* H. VON MANGOLDT & F. KLEIN, DAS BONNER GRUNDGESETZ 2043 f. (Berlin-Frankfurt, Vahlen, 1969).

A similar power is vested in the President of the United States. His veto power, though not restricted to constitutional issues, may be employed when he considers a bill unconstitutional. B. BAKER & S.H. FRIEDELBAUM, GOVERNMENT IN THE UNITED STATES 230 (Boston-New York, Houghton Mifflin, 1966).

and Parliament—which the Constitutional Court has ultimate authority to resolve; thus "political" control, exercised by the President of the Republic, might ultimately come under review by a body which, as we shall see, is judicial in character.[18]

§ 4. Political control of constitutionality: the Soviet Union

Judicial review is lacking in the socialist legal systems, but for reasons very different from those which led to its rejection in France. The French rejected the doctrine essentially because judicial interference in the legislative process was thought to conflict with proper separation of powers. In the Soviet Union and other socialist countries, on the other hand, judicial review was repudiated as one aspect of the "bourgeois doctrine" of the separation of powers. All powers are united in one supreme organ drawn directly from the people, who are "the source of all power."[19] Thus the laws which emanate from the supreme organ (Supreme Soviet, Popular Assembly), whose members are popularly elected, represent "the will of the whole sovereign people."[20] Accordingly, from the principles of the unity of powers and the supremacy of the people flows the corollary that, under socialist systems, constitutional control may not be exercised by extra-parliamentary bodies nor modelled on the experience of West European countries and the United States.[21]

---

[18] Similarly in Germany. *See* VON MANGOLDT & KLEIN, *supra* note 17, at 2043 f.

[19] On the principle of the unity of powers and its applications in the U.S.S.R. see, for example, R. DAVID, LES GRANDS SYSTÈMES DE DROIT CONTEMPORAINS (DROIT COMPARÉ) 228 ff. (Paris, Dalloz, 3d ed. 1969). On the development of the principle under the new Yugoslav Constitution, see J.-P. Ferretjans, *La Constitution du 7 avril 1963 de la République socialiste de Yougoslavie et l'unité marxiste du pouvoir d'état*, 79 REVUE DU DROIT PUBLIC ET DE LA SCIENCE POLITIQUE EN FRANCE ET À L'ÉTRANGER 939, 942 ff. (1963).

[20] A.Y. VYSHINSKY, THE LAW OF THE SOVIET STATE 337 f. (New York, Macmillan, 1961); Vasil'ev, in TEORIJA GOSUDARSTVA I PRAVA 372 (K.A. Mokichev (ed.), Moskva, Juridicheskaja Literatura, 1965); A.F. Shebanov, under *Zakon*, in ENTSIKLOPEDICHESKIJ SLOVAR' PRAVOVYKH ZNANIJ (SOVETSKOE PRAVO) 133 (V.M. Chkhikvadze, *et al.* (eds.), Moskva, Izd. Sovetskaja Entsiklopedija, 1965).

[21] Rozmaryn, *La Constitution, loi fondamentale de l'Etat socialiste*, in P. BISCARETTI DI RUFFÌA & S. ROZMARYN, LA CONSTITUTION COMME LOI FONDAMENTALE DANS LES ETATS DE L'EUROPE OCCIDENTALE ET DANS LES ETATS SOCIALISTES 107 f. (Torino & Paris, Giappichelli & Librairie Générale de Droit et de Jurisprudence, 1966); Kastari, *Le caractère normatif et la prééminence hiérarchique des constitutions*, 18 REVUE INTERNATIONALE DE DROIT COMPARÉ 843, 845 f. (1966). For a criticism of judicial review in the United States from the standpoint of the Soviets see VYSHINSKY, *supra* note 20, at 339 f.

This does not mean, however, that the constitutions of the various socialist countries ignore the problem of control of constitutionality. On the contrary they recognize it, and resolve it in a manner compatible with the fundamental principles of their system.[22] Let us take for example the present Constitution of the U.S.S.R., enacted on December 5, 1936. Article 14 provides: "The competence of the Union of Soviet Socialist Republics, represented by its supreme organs of State power and by the organs of State administration, shall include: . . . d) control over the observance of the Constitution of the U.S.S.R. and guarantee of the conformity of the Constitutions of the Union Republics with the Constitution

---

[22] One must not forget that even the concept of "constitution" is different in Western and Eastern thought. In Western Europe the constitution is conceived as a body of more or less permanent rules and principles which express the fundamental value norms of the state and establish a program for their realization. The situation is different in the U.S.S.R. and other socialist countries. There the constitution, conceived as a superstructure over the economy, reflects socio-economic results achieved. It aims at describing, not prescribing, the actual phase of a socio-economic order in action. See Beér, *The Normative Character of the Constitution of the Hungarian People's Republic*, in 2 ACTA JURIDICA ACADEMIAE SCIENTIARUM HUNGARICAE 246 f. (1960, No. 3/4); Kastari, *supra* note 21, at 843 f.; Ferretjans, *supra* note 19, at 940 ff., and in particular Mouskhély, *La notion soviétique de constitution*, 61 REVUE DU DROIT PUBLIC ET DE LA SCIENCE POLITIQUE EN FRANCE ET À L'ÉTRANGER 894 ff., esp. 897 f. (1955), which quotes Stalin, according to whom the Soviet Constitution does not consist of a program of future attainments but of a "record and legislative consecration of conquests already achieved." See also Azzariti, *I vari sistemi di sindacato sulla costituzionalità delle leggi nei diversi paesi*, in LA CORTE COSTITUZIONALE (RACCOLTA DI STUDI) 14 f. (supplement of LA RASSEGNA MENSILE DELL'AVVOCATURA DELLO STATO, Roma, Istituto Poligrafico dello Stato, 1957). Note, however, the remarks of Biscaretti di Ruffìa, *Quelques considérations finales sur les différentes significations et valeurs de la Constitution en Europe occidentale et dans les Etats socialistes européens*, in BISCARETTI DI RUFFÌA & ROZMARYN, *supra* note 21, at 125 f.; and those of Rozmaryn, *Quelques questions de la théorie des constitutions socialistes*, in 2 LIBER AMICORUM BARON LOUIS FREDERICQ 881 ff., esp. 883 f. (Gent, E. Story-Scientia, 1966). Thus the constitution in the "material" sense and in the "formal" sense, that is to say, the situation determined by the actual dominant political forces on the one hand and on the other the written code of fundamental law, ought faithfully to reflect each other. From this fact, however, there arises the possibility that a decree or enactment may, at a given moment, change the existing socio-economic structure, and that the constitution may be formally amended only later, when the change already effected is solemnly ratified under the agreed procedure for constitutional revision.

On the procedure for the revision of the constitution in socialist countries see Rozmaryn, *supra* note 21, at 114-18; Biscaretti di Ruffìa, *supra*, at 123 f., who also mentions the lax adherence to the formal requirements of the amending process. This practice is, however, criticised by I.N. KUZNETSOV, ZAKONODATEL'NAJA I ISPOL'NITEL'NAJA DEJATEL'NOST' VYSSHIKH ORGANOV VLASTI 120 (Moskva, Juridicheskaja Literatura, 1965). He observes that every modification, even the slightest one, ought to be introduced by the Supreme Soviet itself.

of the U.S.S.R."[23] This is the only provision the Soviet Constitution makes for the review of constitutionality[24] and from it one can deduce which bodies are endowed with the function of review. When speaking of the "supreme organs of State power," article 14 certainly refers to the Supreme Soviet of the U.S.S.R. (the organ roughly comparable to the Parliament of Western countries) and to its Presidium (a collective body composed of 33 members elected from the Soviet itself). The Presidium, in the intervals between the very short sessions of the Supreme Soviet, exercises the latter's

---

[23] Translation supplied from the revised text of the Soviet Constitution published in Moscow, 1965. KONSTITUTSIJA (OSNOVNOJ ZAKON) SOJUZA SOVETSKIKH SOTSIALISTICHESKIKH RESPUBLIK (Moskva, Izvestija sovetov deputatov trudjashchikhsja SSSR, 1965). An English translation of the Constitution of the U.S.S.R. is given by A.J. PEASLEE, 3 CONSTITUTIONS OF NATIONS (The Hague, Nijhoff, 1968).

[24] It seems interesting to mention in this context the terms of art. 49(f) of the current Soviet Constitution. This article gives the Presidium of the Supreme Soviet of the Union the additional power to annul "ordinances and orders of the Council of Ministers of the U.S.S.R. and of the Councils of Ministers of the Republics of the Union, if they do not conform to law." Since the Constitution of the U.S.S.R. is certainly itself a "law," theoretically an enactment of the Council of Ministers could be annulled by the Presidium because of its unconstitutionality. However, there seem to be no precedents for such a case. M. MOUSKHÉLY & Z. JEDRYKA, LE GOUVERNEMENT DE L'U.R.S.S. 172 (Paris, Presses Universitaires de France, 1961), say that Soviet writers do not mention any precedent. Article 49, however, is not specifically intended to cover breaches of constitutionality in the acts of the Councils of Ministers but, much more generally, breaches of legality; protection of the Constitution, in other words, would thus be only incidental.

The control of constitutionality prescribed by the current Constitution of the U.S.S.R., which we have briefly outlined in the text, is somewhat different from the system provided by the former Constitution of 1923. According to this Constitution, control of constitutionality still had a political nature, for it resided in a political body, viz. the Central Executive Committee of the U.S.S.R., the equivalent of the modern Supreme Soviet. Nevertheless, under the 1923 Constitution there also existed a control over constitutionality entrusted to a judicial organ. Article 43 of that Constitution endowed the Supreme Tribunal of the U.S.S.R. with the function of giving "its own opinion, at the request of the Central Executive Committee of the U.S.S.R., on the constitutionality of decrees of the Republics of the Union." The final decision, however, rested always with the Central Executive Committee, which was not bound by the opinion of the Supreme Tribunal. On this, consult id. at 170 f.; S. CATINELLA, LA CORTE SUPREMA FEDERALE NEL SISTEMA COSTITUZIONALE DEGLI STATI UNITI D'AMERICA 126-29 (Padova, Cedam, 1934); Azzariti, supra note 22, at 13 f.; Battaglini, supra note 4, at 715-20.

powers including that of control over constitutionality.[25] The "organs of State administration," referred to in article 14, may be identified under articles 64 and 72 of the Soviet Constitution as the Council of Ministers of the U.S.S.R. and the individual Ministers of the U.S.S.R., appointed by the Supreme Soviet.[26]

Given the terms of article 14 and the clearly political nature of the organs endowed with the task of safeguarding the Constitution, it would seem right to infer, as others have done,[27] the political, not judicial, character of the control itself.[28] The scope of this con-

---

[25] On the powers, in the context of the review of constitutionality, attributed to the Presidium of the Supreme Soviet see MOUSKHÉLY & JEDRYKA, *supra* note 24, at 172; Mitskevich, in OBSHAJA TEORIJA SOVETSKOGO PRAVA 143 f. (S.N. Bratus' & I.S. Samoshchenko (eds.), Moskva, Juridicheskaja Literatura, 1966). *See also* Shorina, in PRAVOVYE GARANTII ZAKONNOSTI V SSSR 60 (M.S. Strogovich (ed.), Moskva, Akademia Nauk SSSR, 1962). She recalls an interesting case of review on the part of the Presidium of the Supreme Soviet over the Constitution of the Soviet Socialist Republic of Moldavia, when art. 113 of this Constitution was held to be contrary to arts. 134 and 135 of the Federal Constitution. As a result, the offending article was duly amended. This occurred in 1948.

For a Soviet criticism about the brevity of the sessions of the U.S.S.R. Supreme Soviet (usually 3 or 4 days, only twice a year) see Shafir, *Organizatsija raboty Verkhovnogo Soveta SSSR i ee pravovoe zakreplenie,* 10 (No. 3) PRAVOVEDENIE 20 f. (1966).

[26] *See* A. DENISOV & M. KIRICHENKO, SOVIET STATE LAW 247 (Moscow, Foreign Languages Publishing House, 1960). On the election of the Council of Ministers by the Supreme Soviet see art. 56 of the Soviet Constitution.

[27] *See* Battaglini, *supra* note 4, at 721; *see also* authors cited note 29 *infra*.

[28] That the socialist countries, with the single exception of Yugoslavia, do not entrust either ordinary judges or a special judicial court with the power of judicial review, is emphasized by Rozmaryn, *supra* note 21, at 107 ff. This writer, however, aptly points out that this situation is relevant only for laws coming into force after the 1936 Constitution, not for anterior laws ("lois préconstitutionnelles") which, if contrary to the Constitution, were abrogated automatically under the precept "lex posterior derogat legi priori" (*Id.* at 100 f., 109). Nevertheless, Rozmaryn at 110 f. mentions that in socialist countries there is no dearth of opinions, both among jurists and even some politicians, favoring the introduction of judicial review; and that the recent Rumanian Constitution of 1965, although not admitting a *judicial* control such as that adopted in 1963 in Yugoslavia (see Ch. III, § 2 *infra*), has instituted within Parliament itself a "Constitutional Committee," elected by Parliament: up to a maximum of a third of the total number of its members, the Committee may be composed of specialists who are not members of Parliament. The Committee under art. 53 of the Constitution has the task of putting before the "Great National Assembly" reports and opinions on the constitutionality of bills, on its own initiative or at the request of the bodies indicated by the rules of Parliamentary procedure. Rozmaryn adds that he would see, *de jure condendo,* no doctrinal or political obstacle, in socialist countries, to granting such a consultative function to the Supreme Court, rather than to a committee nominated by Parliament, for in such a case there would still be no infringement upon the sovereignty of the supreme representative organ. *Id.* at 111. In support of the idea of setting up such a Constitutional Committee in Hungary see Kovács, *Les sources du droit de la République Populaire Hongroise,* 19 REVUE INTERNATIONALE DE DROIT COMPARÉ 674 (1967). Though

trol would, therefore, be to guide the political organs and individuals along the paths set by the Constitution, until such time as the latter shall have been superseded and therefore become susceptible of revision.[29]

Nor is this nonjudicial character of the control the only peculiarity which the Soviet constitutional system presents. There is another which seems to be of interest. Article 14 of the Constitution of 1936, as we have seen, does not limit the function of control to particular categories of acts. Thus, nothing prevents this control from being exercised over all law-creating acts. Nevertheless, one should note a peculiar situation which, in this context, occurs in the Soviet Union. There is a multiplicity of bodies endowed with legislative powers, with the result that it is no easy task to draw a clear picture of the various sources of law,[30] or of their relative hierarchical relationship which the Soviet commentators themselves often fail to

---

a Western nation, Finland has a similar Constitutional Committee within its Parliament. The Finnish Committee, composed of seventeen members of the legislature, must review any constitutional questions which arise in legislation under consideration. In so doing, the Committee normally consults outside experts. The decision of the Committee, unlike that of its Rumanian counterpart, is binding on the legislature, and thus resembles the French *Conseil Constitutionnel. See* Saario, *Control of the Constitutionality of Laws in Finland,* 12 AM. J. COMP. L. 194 ff. (1963).

For very recent developments in Czechoslovakia see Ch. III, text and note 20 *infra.*

[29] *See,* on the same lines, MOUSKHÉLY & JEDRYKA, *supra* note 24, at 170-73; Mouskhély, *supra* note 22, at 906-08. It is true that formal revision of the Constitution demands a particular procedure within the competence of the Supreme Soviet, so that even the Soviet Constitution may be said to be rigid. However, in practice, since amongst the organs of control there are the Council of Ministers and individual ministers, in addition to the Presidium, these bodies may decide that the formal Constitution no longer accords with the economic situation of the moment; in such a case they can pass enactments contrary to the Constitution itself, and these enactments will later be submitted for approval—in practice never refused—to the Supreme Soviet. Revision of the Constitution in the formal sense will thus be effected by the Supreme Soviet after an adaptation effected by other bodies. For an exemplary account of this procedure see P. BISCARETTI DI RUFFÌA, LINEAMENTI GENERALI DELL'ORDINAMENTO COSTITUZIONALE SOVIETICO 87 f. n.113 (Milano, Giuffrè, 1956); R. DAVID, LES DONNÉES FONDAMENTALES DU DROIT SOVIÉTIQUE, Tome 1 of R. DAVID & J.N. HAZARD, LE DROIT SOVIÉTIQUE 226 n.7 (Paris, Librairie Générale de Droit et de Jurisprudence, 1954); R. MAURACH, HANDBUCH DER SOWJETVERFASSUNG 174 (München, Isaac Verlag, 1955); Gsovski, *The Soviet Union,* in 1 GOVERNMENT, LAW AND COURTS IN THE SOVIET UNION AND EASTERN EUROPE 22 ff. (V. Gsovski & K. Grzybowski (eds.), London, Stevens & Sons, 1959); Zellweger, *The Principle of Socialist Legality,* 5 (No. 2) JOURNAL OF THE INTERNATIONAL COMMISSION OF JURISTS 193 f. (1964). This point is explicitly made by Rozmaryn, *supra* note 21, at 114 n.24.

[30] *See* DAVID, *supra* note 29, at 225 ff.; BISCARETTI DI RUFFÌA, *supra* note 29, at 85 ff.

clarify.[31] For our purposes, however, it will suffice to observe that
legislation in the Soviet State is drawn from three principal sources:
(1) "Laws," ratified by the Supreme Soviet of the U.S.S.R.; (2)
"Decrees," emanating from the Presidium of the Supreme Soviet;
(3) "Orders," emanating from the Council of Ministers of the
U.S.S.R.[32] Thus we can see that the organs to which article 14(d)
entrusts, among other tasks, the function of reviewing the constitutionality of law-creating acts, are essentially the same organs (the
Supreme Soviet, the Presidium, and the Council of Ministers of the
U.S.S.R.), from which these acts emanate. Thus control of constitutionality in the Soviet Union is not external, as is typical elsewhere, but internal to the major policy-making bodies of the state.
The body controlled and the body controlling are either the same
or, at least, very closely related (the Presidium and the Council
of Ministers in the U.S.S.R. are, as we have said, elected by the
Supreme Soviet).[33]

§ 5. Political control of constitutionality: possibilities of evolution

Before too sharp a line is drawn between political and judicial
means of controlling the constitutionality of legislation, it should
be noted that even political entities may evolve into something
quite different than that intended by their founders. An example
would be the development of the French *Cassation*. This institution,

---

[31] See MOUSKHÉLY & JEDRYKA, *supra* note 24, at 216, for references to
certain Soviet studies which have dealt with the subject. *See also* Khalfina,
*O problematike teorii gosudarstva i prava v svjazi s zadachei sovershenstvo-
vanija zakonodatel'stva*, 1964 (No. 9) SOVETSKOE GOSUDARSTVO I PRAVO 46 ff.;
Loeber, *Legal Rules "For Internal Use Only,"* 19 INT'L. & COMP. L.Q. 70, 74
ff. (1970).

[32] Laws have the highest position. *See* Vasil'ev, *supra* note 20, at 372, 376.

[33] *See* P. BISCARETTI DI RUFFÌA, INTRODUZIONE AL DIRITTO COSTITUZIONALE
COMPARATO 502 (Milano, Giuffrè, 1969). It is, however, necessary to emphasize
that such a situation may well be the only one compatible with the fundamental principles of a Communist system. Given that the will of the people,
expressed in the body which emanates from it (the Supreme Soviet in the
U.S.S.R., the Popular Assembly or National Assembly elsewhere), represents the
supreme source of law, there is no body, except for this organ itself, which
can be given the task of control over the constitutional legitimacy of its activities. *See* Shorina, *supra* note 25, at 62. This can explain why the same situation
as in the U.S.S.R. arises in the other People's Republics, with the sole exception of Yugoslavia. *See* the detailed country by country analysis of Battaglini,
supra note 4, at 722-50. *See also* Biscaretti di Ruffìa, *La Constitution, en tant
que loi fondamentale, en Europe occidentale*, in BISCARETTI DI RUFFÌA & ROZ-
MARYN, *supra* note 21, at 71. Yugoslavia, alone among the various socialist
states, has recently introduced a system of judicial review, as we shall see in
Chapter III *infra*.

despite its modern purely judicial nature, was originally conceived as a nonjudicial organ of control. Indeed, it was the result of a political philosophy which was radically opposed to any possibility of judicial review.

The *Tribunal de Cassation* was set up by the decree of Nov. 27 - Dec. 1, 1790, as a *nonjudicial* organ strictly connected with the legislative power. As the decree itself stated: "il y aura *près du Corps législatif* un Tribunal de Cassation." Its function was to prevent the judicial organs from interfering in the legislative sphere and to ensure that they applied only the letter of the law. This was a phase in the development of the concept which soon resulted in the great French codification, a concept that the entire body of law could and should be contained in written instruments. Despite the name *Tribunal*, which was later changed to "Court" *(Cour)*, the *Tribunal de Cassation* originally had an essentially legislative character; it was a political, rather than a judicial body. In the words of the author of a leading work on *Cassation*, it was "an institution of a constitutional nature intended to preserve in its entirety that tenet of the separation of powers," which was held to be "the prime condition for the normal existence of the State."[34] In view of its functions, there was a proposal to call it, instead of *Tribunal de Cassation, Conseil national pour la conservation des lois*—a name certainly more descriptive of its original task.

The *Tribunal de Cassation,* in short, was the offspring of the revolutionary legislators' profound distrust of the judges. In the first years of the Revolution, this distrust led them to emulate Justinian in attempting to deny the judges all power to interpret the laws out of fear that through interpretation the literal meaning of a law might be changed. The power of interpretation was reserved to the legislative body, by means of decrees issued at the request of the judges whenever they were in doubt as to the meaning of a legis-

---

[34] P. CALAMANDREI, 1 LA CASSAZIONE CIVILE 448 (Torino, Bocca, 1920). It has been shown that the French version of cassation had a precedent in the medieval *querela nullitatis* (a form of attacking judgments). *See* P. Calamandrei, under *Cassazione civile*, in 2 NUOVO DIGESTO ITALIANO 986 f. (Torino, UTET, 1937). *See also* E. GLASSON & A. TISSIER, 1 TRAITÉ THÉORIQUE ET PRATIQUE D'ORGANISATION JUDICIAIRE, DE COMPÉTENCE ET DE PROCÉDURE CIVILE 253 ff. (Paris, Sirey, 3d ed. 1925).

lative text.[35] Only by the Napoleonic Code were this so-called *référé facultatif* and the utopian prohibition of judicial interpretation abolished.[36]

The doctrine of the separation of powers was likewise strictly applied to prevent legislative interference with the judicial power. Thus the *Tribunal de Cassation*, although able to annul, at the request of a private citizen (or even, without such a request, "in the interest of the law"), judgments which contained "an express contravention of the text of the law," had to restrict itself rigidly to this task. It was "not to usurp judicial functions which are not its concern;" it had no power to "pronounce upon the interpretation of the laws or upon the decision in the dispute."[37] For the new decision in the dispute, the *Tribunal de Cassation* remanded the case to the so-called "juridiction de renvoi," that is, to a different lower court which had complete freedom of decision and could even defy *Cassation* by reinstating the previous decision. The only limitation was that, if the second decision was again brought before the *Tribunal de Cassation* and again quashed by it, and if the second "juridiction de renvoi" persisted with the opinion held illegal by the Cassation, the so-called *référé obligatoire* before the *Corps législatif* became necessary. The legislative body then published a decree, declaratory of the law, which bound the courts on the third "renvoi."[38]

Had *Cassation* not undergone profound changes during the nearly two centuries of its history, it would be difficult to imagine a more irreconcilable contrast between the ideas at the base of that institution and those which have inspired all systems of judicial

---

[35] "Ils [les tribunaux] ne pourront point faire des règlements, mais ils s'addresseront au Corps législatif toutes les fois qu'ils croiront nécessaire soit d'interpréter une loi, soit d'en faire une nouvelle," art. 12, title II, law of August 16-24, 1790.

For an examination of the article in question and of the various stages in its final elaboration, see the interesting study of Y.-L. HUFTEAU, LE RÉFÉRÉ LÉGISLATIF ET LES POUVOIRS DU JUGE DANS LE SILENCE DE LA LOI, esp. 29 ff. (Paris, Presses Universitaires de France, 1965).

[36] *Id.* at 50 ff.

[37] Calamandrei, under *Cassazione civile, supra* note 34, at 988 f.

[38] ". . . Mais lorsque le jugement aura été cassé deux fois, et qu'un troisième tribunal aura jugé en dernier ressort, de la même manière que les deux premiers, la question ne pourra plus être agitée au Tribunal de Cassation qu'elle n'ait été soumise au Corps législatif, qui, en ce cas, portera un décrêt déclaratoire de la loi; et lorsque ce décrêt aura été sanctionné par le Roi, le Tribunal de Cassation s'y conformera dans son jugement." Second part of art. 21 of the law of Nov. 27-Dec. 1, 1790. In this context see HUFTEAU, *supra* note 35, at 40 ff., 43.

review of legislation. For *Cassation* was, in a sense, the embodiment of the concept of the strictest separation of powers under which "law is law" and not what judges may think to be law. Judicial review, on the contrary, presupposes that the judiciary not only has the power of interpretation beyond the strict letter of the law, but, even more importantly, is entitled to rule upon the validity of ordinary legislation, deciding upon its conformity with the higher law. *Cassation* assumed the omnipotence of positive law as the manifestation of the supreme will of popular assemblies; judicial review requires the subjection of the ordinary law to a *lex superior* withdrawn from the vagaries of parliamentary majorities. Finally, the former institution presupposed a profound mistrust of the judiciary[39] while the latter presumes a great confidence in it, if not even its "supremacy" in the constitutional organization of the State.[40]

In fact, by the beginning of the 19th century the attenuation of strict revolutionary ideology was radically transforming the nature of the *Tribunal de Cassation*, by this time called *Cour de Cassation*. In this changed role *Cassation* penetrated to a number of countries, including Italy, Belgium, the Netherlands, Luxembourg, Greece, Spain, and Mexico. Once the judges' power to interpret the law had been recognized by the Napoleonic Code, the *Cour de Cassation* became the supreme *judicial* organ for the review of errors of law committed by inferior judges. The *référé obligatoire* was finally abolished by a law of April 1, 1837, and it was declared that in case of a difference on a point of law between the first *juridiction de renvoi* and the *Cour de Cassation*, the new judgment of the Court, sitting in joint session, should have not only the negative effect of annulment, but also the positive effect of binding the second *juridiction de renvoi*.[41] After the law of April 1, 1837,

---

[39] Even today an authoritative French jurist writes, "la France s'est, depuis la Révolution, toujours défiée du juge." G. Vedel, *Préface* to BATAILLER, *supra* note 6, at II.

[40] A well-known French work on the theory of the judges' "supremacy" deriving from their power of controlling the validity of legislation is E. LAMBERT, LE GOUVERNEMENT DES JUGES ET LA LUTTE CONTRE LA LÉGISLATION SOCIALE AUX ETATS-UNIS (Paris, Giard, 1921).

[41] "Lorsque après la cassation d'un premier arrêt ou jugement rendu en dernier ressort, le deuxième arrêt ou jugement rendu dans la même affaire entre les mêmes parties procédant de la même qualité est attaqué par les mêmes moyens que le premier, la chambre compétente saisit les Chambres réunies par un arrêt de renvoi." "Si le deuxième arrêt ou jugement est cassé pour les mêmes motifs que le premier, la juridiction à laquelle l'affaire est renvoyée doit se conformer à la décision de la Cour de Cassation sur le point de droit jugé par cette Cour." Arts. 1 and 2 of the law of April 1, 1837. These provisions, as contained in articles 58 and 60 of the law of July 23, 1947, are still in force. *See* HUFTEAU, *supra* note 35, at 131 ff.

"more and more decisively and consciously, the Court of Cassation became what it is today, the Supreme Court for the judicial interpretation of the law."[42] Thus it became the Court exercising that control of legality which, although not being by any means the same thing, yet is neither irreconcilable with, nor unrelated to, control of the constitutionality of legislation.[43]

§ 6. Judicial control of constitutionality: general

Just as there are many possible political controls over arbitrary state action, so there are many different ways in which the judiciary might attain the same end. Even a court without the authority to annul unconstitutional legislation might, through rules of interpretation, application of "unwritten principles," and careful control of administrative acts, achieve a form of control of constitutionality. An example of such "implied" control would be that exercised by the French *Conseil d'Etat*. Other courts, rather than focusing on the unconstitutional statute, will provide special forms of relief for individuals who complain of violations of "fundamental rights" by any branch of the government. These remedies may exist independently of any formal system of judicial review of statutes (one aspect of habeas corpus in Great Britain), or in conjunction with judicial review of legislation (one aspect of habeas corpus in the United States), or may specifically exclude the possibility of annulling a statute (one interpretation of *juicio de amparo* in Mexico). Yet, to the average citizen, these procedures might be a more meaningful guarantee of his rights than judicial review itself. In the interest of placing judicial review in this larger context, some of these alternative methods of judicial control will be cursorily discussed.

§ 7. Judicial control of constitutionality: the Conseil d'Etat

Although France has not thus far allowed its judiciary to pass openly upon the constitutionality of statutes, that country has none-

---

[42] Calamandrei, under *Cassazione civile, supra* note 34, at 989.

[43] This point may be demonstrated by Mexican legal history. The institution of *casación* had also penetrated to that country but was later absorbed by the *juicio de amparo*. The latter now performs the functions both of the control of

theless been affected by the same events which have touched so much of the world. The Vichy régime shook France's faith in the popular legislature and since the 1940's the French have gradually altered their conception of separation of powers.[44] Thus the Constitution of 1958 placed many traditionally legislative functions in the hands of the executive, designating the *Conseil Constitutionnel* as an organ of political control over parliamentary attempts to reclaim these functions.[45] The limitations of this form of control have been noted:[46] it does not allow for party initiative; it does not permit review of executive acts—even of those legislative in nature —for their conformity with the Constitution; nor may the *Conseil Constitutionnel* pass upon statutes after they have been promulgated.

The *Conseil d'Etat*, traditionally charged with reviewing abuses of administrative action, has attempted to fill this vacuum, and in so doing has evolved an effective, if incomplete, control mechanism. Before Vichy, a challenged administrative action could be reviewed by the *Conseil* only for its conformity with the enabling statute. Even if the act were unconstitutional, it could not be attacked if authorized by statute.[47] The first break in this tradition came toward the end of the Vichy period when it became clear that the *Conseil d'Etat* would review administrative acts not only for conformity with the statute but also for conformity with the

---

the legality of inferior judgments and of judicial review of legislation. *See* Fix Zamudio, *supra* note 3, at 258 ff., 381 ff.

[44] The Vichy régime, according to many, stimulated the courts to begin this change by leaving them a simple choice: either they could acquiesce in the new concept of governmental power and individual rights, or they could recognize the Vichy abuses as temporary aberrations from the main principles of French tradition, to be narrowly construed and rendered unenforceable if at all possible. *Cf.* Boulanger, *Principes généraux du droit et droit positif,* in Etudes Ripert, Le droit privé français au milieu du XXe siècle 51-74 (Paris, Pichon et Durand-Auzias, 1950).

[45] Note especially arts. 34, 37, 61 and 62 of the Constitution of 1958, and see Geck, *supra* note 1, at 271 ("the 'Conseil Constitutionnel' is mainly tailored to protect the constitutional powers of the executive against Parliament").

[46] See § 2 *supra.*

[47] *See generally* Letourneur, *Les principes généraux du droit dans la jurisprudence du Conseil d'Etat,* in 1951 Conseil d'Etat—Etudes et Documents 19 ff.

"general principles of law," these principles being derived from the Constitution and the Declaration of the Rights of Man.[48]

The second great expansion of the *Conseil's* power of review was occasioned by the passage of the 1958 Constitution which radically extended the administration's power to promulgate regulations clearly legislative in nature. If there were to be no check on the legality of the exercise of this power, the "Government could do anything in its domain; its powers would be unlimited."[49] Yet if these quasi-legislative enactments were to be nullifiable for failure to conform with the Constitution or the "general principles," the *Conseil d'Etat* would have come near to assuming the power to invalidate statutes per se. The *Conseil* has, in fact, taken the latter course: all executive acts, decrees, and ordinances, even those legislative in nature, will be reviewed in adversary, party-initiated proceedings for conformity with applicable statutes, the provisions of the Constitution, and the "general principles of law."

The evolution of the *Conseil d'Etat* is not yet complete. It has yet to refuse recognition to a statute which clearly authorizes an unconstitutional administrative act. But its tendency to "interpret away" statutory provisions of questionable constitutionality,[50] its reading of the general principles into all statutes, its willingness to give damages even in cases where the act complained of has been

---

[48] See as examples of the philosophy implied in the concept of "principes généraux," the following decisions:

(a) *Couitéas, Conseil d'Etat,* 30 November 1923, as reported in LES GRANDS ARRÊTS DE LA JURISPRUDENCE ADMINISTRATIVE 177 ff. (M. Long, P. Weil & G. Braibant (eds.), Paris, Sirey, 4th ed. 1965) (equality before public exactions, *i.e.,* "charges publics");

(b) *Société du Journal "L'Aurore", Conseil d'Etat,* 25 June 1948, as reported *id.* (4th ed. 1965) at 300 ff. (nonretroactivity of administrative decisions);

(c) *Chaveneau, Conseil d'Etat,* 1 April 1949, as reported *id.* (3d ed. 1962) at 304 ff. (liberty of conscience);

(d) *Barel, Conseil d'Etat,* 28 May 1954, as reported *id.* (4th ed. 1965) at 407 ff. (freedom of opinion).

[49] *Syndicat général des ingenieurs-conseils, Conseil d'Etat,* 26 June 1959, as reported in 1959 RECUEIL DALLOZ (JURISPRUDENCE) 541 ff., and in LES GRANDS ARRÊTS DE LA JURISPRUDENCE ADMINISTRATIVE (4th ed. 1965), *supra* note 48, at 466 ff.

[50] *Lamotte, Conseil d'Etat,* 17 Feb. 1950, as reported in LES GRANDS ARRÊTS DE LA JURISPRUDENCE ADMINISTRATIVE (4th ed. 1965), *supra* note 48, at 325 ff.

authorized by statute,[51] and its careful review of quasi-legislative ordinances and decrees constitute a formidable array of weapons. These, together with the political controls of the *Conseil Constitutionnel*, offer a measure of the French response to arguments for some sort of effective control over the constitutionality of legislation.

§ 8. Judicial control of constitutionality: special remedies

The remedies described below, though products of three highly disparate cultures, share several striking similarities. All constitute a recognition that certain individual rights are so important that extraordinary procedural means must be available should they be violated. Yet the special character of all three has been threatened by attempts to make them available as means of reviewing questions of lesser importance. Finally, all three procedures have acquired an unusually high esteem in their countries of origin, an esteem which may even exceed that of formal review of statutes.

a) *Habeas Corpus:* The "Great Writ," "the highest remedy for any man that is imprisoned,"[52] began as a simple command from the Crown to an official, a command most frequently used by the courts at Westminster to secure jurisdiction over persons detained by lower courts. But as the monarchy asserted its right to imprison any person without trial "upon Her Majesty's special commandment,"[53] the courts used the writ to bring before them all those "not obviously committed by lawful means" (the Habeas Corpus Act of 1679). Thus the individual was assured of a hearing to determine whether or not he had been restrained by due process. In this way, the Irish patriot, Wolfe Tone, was freed (1789) in order that he might be given a common law trial (his previous court-martial being declared inadequate).[54]

---

[51] *See* Note by M. Fromont in 1962 RECUEIL DALLOZ (JURISPRUDENCE) 425 ff.

[52] T.F.T. PLUCKNETT, A CONCISE HISTORY OF THE COMMON LAW 58 (Boston, Little, Brown and Co., 5th ed. 1956). "The writ is applicable as a remedy in all cases of wrongful deprivation of personal liberty. Where the detention of an individual is under process for criminal or supposed criminal causes the jurisdiction of the Court and the regularity of the commitment may be inquired into." 11 HALSBURY'S LAWS OF ENGLAND 24 (Simonds (ed.), London, Butterworth, 3d ed. 1955).

[53] PLUCKNETT, *supra* note 52, at 58.

[54] *Id.* at 57-59.

The United States Constitution (art. I, § 9, clause 2) recognized the importance of the writ and forbade its suspension save in time of rebellion or invasion. Today habeas corpus remains the most important means of challenging unconstitutional and otherwise illegal detentions. Its advantages are many, and not least among them is the fact that it tends to precipitate judicial inquiry into the alleged violation of right.[55] In the pretrial stage, the writ has been used to challenge the sufficiency of charges made against the prisoner, the existence of probable cause for such charges, refusal to set bail, and the legality of extradition or interstate rendition proceedings. It may also be used to challenge administrative orders resulting in the detainment or deportation of an asserted alien. After trial, it may be used to obtain relief collateral to that available through normal appeal procedures.[56] For example, a defendant imprisoned without having had adequate legal representation will be able to assert his claim via habeas corpus after the normal time for appeal has run.[57]

The Great Writ continues to evolve. Most recently it has become a weapon against state claims that failure by a defendant to follow all state procedures will result in his being unable to vindicate his fundamental rights.[58] Some have claimed that the writ has been overly expanded in that, in some cases, it allows a complete rehearing of factual and legal issues already decided.[59] Be that as it may, the use of the writ to vindicate certain higher federal rights, rights which have often been ignored or evaded by less sensitive lower courts, is an important aid in attaining the goals set for judicial review itself.

b) *Amparo contra leyes:* The *juicio de amparo*,[60] as included in the Mexican Constitution of 1857, was probably intended to be an analog of the writ of habeas corpus; nevertheless, due to insufficient

---

[55] H.M. HART & H. WECHSLER, THE FEDERAL COURTS AND THE FEDERAL SYSTEM 55 (Brooklyn, Foundation Press, 1953).

[56] On the uses of the writ *see generally id.* at 1238-40; R.P. SOKOL, FEDERAL HABEAS CORPUS (Charlottesville, Va., Michie Co., 2d ed. 1969); *Developments in the Law—Federal Habeas Corpus,* 83 HARV. L. REV. 1038 (1970).

[57] Gideon v. Wainwright, 372 U.S. 335 (1963).

[58] Fay v. Noia, 372 U.S. 391 (1963).

[59] Townsend v. Sain, 372 U.S. 293 (1963) (dissenting opinion).

[60] The *amparo,* considered to be one of the most characteristic features of the Mexican legal system, has also been introduced in other Latin American countries, although sometimes with doubtful success. *See generally* H. FIX ZAMUDIO, VEINTICINCO AÑOS DE EVOLUCIÓN DE LA JUSTICIA CONSTITUCIONAL 1940-1965, at 19 ff., 156 ff. (México, UNAM-Instituto de Investigaciones Jurídicas, 1968); Eder, *Judicial Review in Latin America,* 21 OHIO ST. L.J. 570 ff., 602 ff. (1960).

knowledge of the writ,[61] as well as to the jurisprudence of the Mexican courts, *amparo* has become something quite different. Whereas habeas corpus has remained pre-eminently the weapon of the illegally detained individual, *amparo* is available to any party whose rights or duties have been violated by any branch of the government. Since under article 14 the right or duty affected need not be specifically included in the Constitution, *amparo* has a dual role: it is a control on *illegal* as well as on *unconstitutional* state action.[62] The petitioner, by alleging personal harm resulting from the challenged government action, and by alleging exhaustion of other remedies, may attack the constitutionality of a statute, judicial interpretations of the law (analogous to the continental *recours en cassation*), or unauthorized administrative acts (similar to the *recours* before the *Conseil d'Etat*).[63] Pending decision, the challenged act may be suspended with regard to the complainant. Following a favorable decision, the act will be annulled vis-à-vis the individual, and the "responsible authority" *(autoridad responsable)* may be liable for damages.[64]

Several factors limit the effectiveness of *amparo* as a check on unconstitutional statutes.[65] First, in order to attack a law or an administrative decision, one must claim that its effects were *direct* and *personal*, i.e., the law or decision must be "self-executing" *(auto-ejecutiva)*. Those laws which require a further exercise of administrative action for their enforcement may not be directly challenged. Second, a decision in *amparo* does not have *erga omnes* effects; the effects of the governmental act may be suspended for the individual petitioner, but other parties in the same situation may not claim the benefits of the decision. Third, and most important, the *juicio de amparo*, being available for minor questions of illegality as well as for major questions of constitutionality, has lost part of its efficacy as an expeditious protection of fundamental rights. Due to the large number of petitions for *amparo*, decisions are often rendered after long delays and perhaps without the care-

---

[61] *See* J.A.C. GRANT, EL CONTROL JURISDICCIONAL DE LA CONSTITUCION-ALIDAD DE LAS LEYES 51 ff. (México, Publicación de la Revista de la Facultad de Derecho de México, 1963).

[62] BURGOA, *supra* note 3, at 163 ff.

[63] GRANT, *supra* note 61, at 66; FIX ZAMUDIO, *supra* note 3, at 241 ff.; A. Ríos ESPINOZA, AMPARO Y CASACIÓN (México, Editorial "Nueva Xochitl," 1960).

[64] M. Cappelletti, under *Amparo*, in 2 ENCICLOPEDIA DEL DIRITTO 329 ff. (Milano, Giuffrè, 1958).

[65] *Id.*

ful consideration to which, if they concern basic liberties, they are entitled.

Regardless of these limitations, the *juicio de amparo* is most significant in the legal system of Mexico and of the other countries which have adopted the institution.[66] It represents an early recognition not only of the supremacy of constitutional rights but also of the need for extraordinary means of protection should these rights be threatened.

c) *Verfassungsbeschwerde:* Though there were historical precedents in Switzerland, Austria, and Bavaria for *Verfassungsbeschwerde* (most closely translated as "constitutional recourse"), this form of judicial control over unconstitutional state action was not included in the 1949 Constitution of the German Federal Republic.[67] Rather, it was adopted by statute in 1951 as an extraordinary recourse available to the individual whose fundamental rights have been directly denied by any statute, judicial decision, or administrative act. It allows him to obtain an expeditious hearing before the Federal Constitutional Court *(Bundesverfassungsgericht)* if he alleges a violation of a *Grundrecht* or other constitutional right of equivalent importance.[68]

The effects of a decision by the Federal Constitutional Court in response to a petition brought under the law of 1951 may be far-reaching. A statute found unconstitutional is declared null. This declaration binds all inferior courts and administrative agencies.[69]

---

[66] See the remarks by a Mexican commentator, Tena Ramírez, *El aspecto mundial del amparo. Su expansión internacional*, in MÉXICO ANTE AL PENSAMIENTO JURÍDICO-SOCIAL DE OCCIDENTE 133 ff., 155 and *passim* (México, Editorial Jus, 1955).

[67] M. CAPPELLETTI, LA GIURISDIZIONE COSTITUZIONALE DELLE LIBERTÀ (Milano, Giuffrè, 1955) discusses the institution of *Verfassungsbeschwerde* in Switzerland, Austria and Germany and that of the Bavarian *Popularklage*. See *also* A.H. SCHULER, DIE VERFASSUNGSBESCHWERDE IN DER SCHWEIZ, DER BUNDESREPUBLIK DEUTSCHLAND UND ÖSTERREICH (Zürich, Schulthess, 1968); Geck, *supra* note 1, at 294 ff.

[68] In particular the German *Verfassungsbeschwerde*, the Swiss *staatsrechtliche Beschwerde (recours de droit public)* and the Bavarian *Popularklage* can, within certain limits, be used also against legislative enactments conflicting with fundamental freedoms. CAPPELLETTI, *supra* note 67, at 25 ff., 69 ff., 81 ff. To some extent these institutions, albeit in a special way, may therefore give rise to judicial control of the constitutionality of legislation. See Engelhardt, *supra* note 9, at 116, 119. See also Ch. III, note 9 *infra*.

[69] *See* BUNDESVERFASSUNGSGERICHTSGESETZ § 31(1) and § 95(3); and references in G. LEIBHOLZ & R. RUPPRECHT, BUNDESVERFASSUNGSGERICHTSGESETZ, RECHTSPRECHUNGSKOMMENTAR 97 ff., 428 ff. (Köln, Otto Schmidt, 1968).

Accordingly, *Verfassungsbeschwerde* allows one to have his constitutionally grounded complaint heard speedily by the Constitutional Court in a direct action concerned solely with the constitutional issue raised. Though there is a requirement of exhaustion of ordinary remedies (unless a self-executing statute is challenged), a party may avoid these often costly and time-consuming procedures by showing that the alleged grievance is of "general importance" or that "grave and irreparable damage" may result from denying an immediate hearing.[70] It must be remembered that many civil law systems do not provide for the immediate equitable relief available in the common law. *Amparo*, as we have seen, attacks the problem by suspending the effects of state action while the federal court's decision is pending. *Verfassungsbeschwerde* accomplishes much the same result both by allowing an allegation of "grave and irreparable damage" and by permitting the Constitutional Court to adopt provisional remedies, with the added advantage that a favorable decision by the Court will annul the invalid act or law not only with regard to the complaining party but also vis-à-vis all others in the same situation.

§ 9. Summary

It is possible to exaggerate the importance of formal judicial review of statutes as a barrier to arbitrary state action. Some states have recognized that in many ways maintaining such a barrier is a political task and accordingly have relied on political institutions to accomplish it. Other states have seen that formal review of statutes may be less important to the citizenry than the provision of immediate relief to the injured party and have instituted remedies like habeas corpus, *amparo*, and *Verfassungsbeschwerde* to afford such relief. Finally, many countries have established a variety of controls, both political and judicial, among which judicial review of legislation plays a key role.

One might ask why the various nations have chosen such widely different means of control since in their recent history all have had somewhat similar experiences. The answer is, as might be expected, historical and philosophical. Both the Soviet Union and France have eschewed judicial means of testing the constitutionality of

---

[70] BUNDESVERFASSUNGSGERICHTSGESETZ § 90(2). T. MAUNZ, H. SIGLOCH, B. SCHMIDT-BLEIBTREU & F. KLEIN, BUNDESVERFASSUNGSGERICHTSGESETZ § 90, at 143 ff. (München-Berlin, Beck, 1967).

legislation. As noted above, however, the reason in one case was an aversion to the whole separation of powers concept, while in the other case it was an extreme commitment to the doctrine of separation, a commitment rooted in early attempts by the judiciary to interfere with the legitimate functions of other branches of the government.

Even within the West there are wide differences in outlook. France learned to be suspicious of its judiciary; the British, on the contrary, came to look to their judges to protect them against government arbitrariness. Germany and Italy, while influenced by 19th century French thought, were forced by the Nazi-Fascist experience to rethink their attitudes toward the legislature. These differences, along with a common western tradition of subordinating "lower" to "higher" norms,[71] will be treated in the following chapters. In light of these factors the choices made by various countries, between political and judicial controls, between "centralized" and "decentralized" control,[72] between review *incidenter* and *principaliter*,[73] and between *erga omnes* and *inter partes* decisions,[74] will become more understandable.

---

[71] See Ch. II *infra*.
[72] See Ch. III *infra*.
[73] See Ch. IV *infra*.
[74] See Ch. V *infra*.

CHAPTER II

HISTORICAL ANTECEDENTS OF JUDICIAL REVIEW

§ 1. Judicial review of legislation: a distinctively American contribution to political theory?

While judicial review as a working method of subordinating state action to higher principles was first effectively implemented in the United States, clearly the idea did not spring new and fully developed from the head of John Marshall. Rather, the American version of judicial review was the logical result of centuries of European thought and colonial experiences, which had made western man in general willing to admit the theoretical primacy of certain kinds of law and had made Americans in particular ready to provide a *judicial* means of enforcing that primacy.[1]

This is not to minimize the importance of the American contribution, since prior to the formation of the American system of judicial review, nothing similar had been created in other countries. The reason for this is readily understandable, as it was the Constitution of the United States which initiated the era of "constitutionalism," with the notion of the supremacy of the constitution over ordinary laws. The American Constitution represented the archetype of so-called "rigid" constitutions in contrast to "flexible" ones. That is to say that it was the model of those constitutions not

---

[1] For a thesis suggesting that judicial review was a distinctively American contribution to political theory see J.A.C. GRANT, EL CONTROL JURISDICCIONAL DE LA CONSTITUCIONALIDAD DE LAS LEYES. UNA CONTRIBUCIÓN DE LAS AMÉRICAS A LA CIENCIA POLÍTICA (Publicación de la Revista de la Facultad de Derecho de México, 1963). *See also* C.J. FRIEDRICH, THE IMPACT OF AMERICAN CONSTITUTIONALISM ABROAD 92 (Boston University Press, 1967) (". . . the basic idea of judicial review is of American origin").

Admittedly any attempt made to find exact historical precedents for judicial review would be a hazardous undertaking. For example, voiding of colonial statutes by the Privy Council as contrary to imperial legislation (§ 5 *infra*), or voiding of a state or local law as violative of a national (federal) constitution, is not the same as voiding of a federal statute by the judiciary as contrary to a federal constitution. Our theme—the influence of higher law ideas in western history, and the use of the judiciary to guarantee this law—applies, however, to all these cases.

subject to change or revision through the ordinary laws, but changeable, if at all, only by a special amending procedure. By way of contrast, the unwritten British Constitution is still flexible,[2] as was the *Statuto Albertino*, the Italian Constitution of 1848, which has been replaced by the rigid Republican Constitution of 1948.

The American Constitution of 1789, on the other hand, expressly declared in article VI, paragraph 2: "This Constitution . . . shall be the supreme Law of the Land; and the Judges in every State shall be bound thereby . . . ." This article, as it has been interpreted, especially through the work of John Marshall, has been of fundamental importance and has brought about radical innovations. On the one hand, it was the source of the supremacy of the Constitution; on the other hand, it led to the power and the duty of the judiciary to disregard laws contrary to the Constitution itself.[3] In this context the judgment of the Supreme Court, rendered in 1803 by Chief Justice Marshall in *Marbury v. Madison*,[4] is well-known. Here the differences between rigid and flexible constitutions and the necessity of choosing between one or the other were expounded with great logical clarity.[5] It is evident, as the judgment declares, that either the constitution prevails over legislative enactments contrary to it, or the legislature is able to change the constitution by ordinary legislation. There is no middle road between these alternatives. Either the constitution is fundamental law, superior and unchangeable by ordinary means, or it is placed on the same level as ordinary legislative enactments and, as a result, can be altered

---

[2] *See, e.g.,* O. HOOD PHILLIPS, CONSTITUTIONAL AND ADMINISTRATIVE LAW 26 (London, Sweet & Maxwell, 4th ed. 1967).

[3] See the chapter on the "Principle of Supremacy" in W.J. WAGNER, THE FEDERAL STATES AND THEIR JUDICIARY 73 ff. (The Hague, Mouton, 1959). Not all would agree that art. VI, para. 2, unequivocally supports those who defend the assumption of the power of constitutional control by the judiciary. The point is still controversial among scholars, though it is now, of course, of only theoretical importance. See A.M. BICKEL, THE LEAST DANGEROUS BRANCH 2-14 (Indianapolis-New York, Bobbs-Merrill, 1962); Wechsler, *Toward Neutral Principles of Constitutional Law*, 73 HARV. L. REV. 1-10 (1959).

[4] 5 U.S. (1 Cranch) 137 (1803).

[5] Some have even said that Marshall's emphasis on logic, to the exclusion of citation to the historical precedents for judicial review, has made it easier for those inimical to judicial review to challenge it as a "usurpation": "If Marshall had made it clear that he was using arguments put forward long before . . ., and if he had shown that he conceived of his task not as demonstrating beyond the palest shadow of a doubt the correctness of the doctrine of judicial review, but rather as establishing that this doctrine had decidedly better claims than its opposite, then perhaps the 'usurpation' myth would have enjoyed less perennial appeal." C.L. BLACK, THE PEOPLE AND THE COURT, JUDICIAL REVIEW IN A DEMOCRACY 26 (Englewood Cliffs, New Jersey, Prentice-Hall, 1960).

at will by the legislative body. If the former alternative is accepted, then one must conclude that a legislative enactment contrary to the constitution is not law; if, on the other hand, the second alternative is chosen, written constitutions are no more than worthless attempts to limit a power which by its very nature is illimitable.

Marshall's decision, with its enunciation of the supremacy of the constitution over other laws and of the judicial power to disregard unconstitutional laws, has certainly been a grand innovation. Today almost all modern constitutions of the western world tend to be rigid rather than flexible;[6] this fundamentally important world-wide movement was effectively begun by the American Constitution of 1789[7] and its courageous interpretation by the Supreme Court.

Yet these developments must be seen not as a denial, but as a fulfillment of the past. For, even without expressly and consciously envisaging "supremacy of the Constitution" over ordinary laws, other and earlier legal systems have provided various forms of supremacy of a certain law or of a given set of laws. These might, in modern terminology, justly be called constitutional or fundamental laws, "Grundgesetze," taking precedence over other laws which, again in modern terminology, might be called ordinary laws. Of course, while much of Western Europe has shared at one time or another in the desire to insure the supremacy of the fundamental law, local experiences have caused different states to look to different means for bringing about this goal. Some, for example, tended to look to the popular legislature to uphold higher principles, while others placed more faith in the judiciary. An examination of these historical similarities (*i.e.*, the common striving toward the definition and enforcement of a higher law) and differences (*i.e.*, as to the faith to be placed in the legislature vis-à-vis the judiciary)

---

[6] The same even applies to all the constitutions of eastern European countries, although (with the sole exception of Yugoslavia) they do not acknowledge judicial control of the constitutionality of legislation (see Ch. I, § 4 *supra*). *See* P. BISCARETTI DI RUFFÌA & S. ROZMARYN, LA CONSTITUTION COMME LOI FONDAMENTALE DANS LES ETATS DE L'EUROPE OCCIDENTALE ET DANS LES ETATS SOCIALISTES *passim*, esp. 114-18, 121 f. (Torino & Paris, Giappichelli & Librairie Générale de Droit et de Jurisprudence, 1966). For the rigid nature of all modern European constitutions, with the sole exception of the British one, and also for the origins of the doctrinal distinction between "flexible" and "rigid" Constitutions see *id.* at 5, 47 ff.

[7] *Cf. id.* at 10, 48, 70. *See also* Azzariti, *I vari sistemi di sindacato sulla costituzionalità delle leggi nei diversi paesi*, in LA CORTE COSTITUZIONALE (RACCOLTA DI STUDI) 4, 20 (supplement of LA RASSEGNA MENSILE DELLA AVVOCATURA DELLO STATO, Roma, Istituto Poligrafico dello Stato, 1957).

would go far toward explaining present day contrasts between various systems of constitutional control.

§ 2.   "Higher law" conceptions in classical antiquity

The belief, then, in the need to subordinate certain acts of the law-making power to higher, more permanent principles is not confined to our own time. It may be traced, through the Enlightenment philosophers, the English courts of equity, the French *Parlements*, the medieval scholastics, and early Church fathers to its earliest direct origins in Greco-Roman civilization.[8]

In Athenian law, for example, there was a distinction made between a *nómos*, corresponding to law in the strict sense, and a *pséphisma*, which in our times might be called a decree. In fact *nómoi* might in a certain sense be compared to modern constitutional laws,[9] for they often concerned the organization of the State and could be amended only by a special procedure which would remind a modern lawyer of the procedure for revision of the Constitution.[10] As a well known student of Attic law has written, there was "a notion common to all the Greek states" that the law or *nómos* ought to be something fixed and "withdrawn from the tumultuous vicissitudes of political life and from the headstrong impulses of the assemblies."[11] Therefore, the procedure devised for amending the *nómoi* in Athens was very complex; revision of the laws was a matter of extreme seriousness and was surrounded by most carefully conceived and unusual guarantees. Heavy responsibility was placed on the person who proposed an amendment which was

---

[8] *See generally* E.S. CORWIN, THE "HIGHER LAW" BACKGROUND OF AMERICAN CONSTITUTIONAL LAW (Ithaca, N.Y., Cornell University Press, 1955, fifth printing, 1963), published in 42 HARV. L. REV. 149 (1928). *See also* M. BATTAGLINI, CONTRIBUTO ALLA STORIA DEL CONTROLLO DI COSTITUZIONALITÀ DELLE LEGGI (Milano, Giuffrè, 1957); R. MARCIC, VERFASSUNG UND VERFASSUNGSGERICHT 177-82 (Wien, Springer Verlag, 1963); L.P. BETH, POLITICS, THE CONSTITUTION AND THE SUPREME COURT 2-14 (Evanston, Ill., Row Peterson, 1962) and the bibliographical references therein; Deener, *Judicial Review in Modern Constitutional Systems*, 46 AM. POL. SCI. REV. 1079 ff. (1952).

[9] *See* U.E. Paoli, under *Nomothetai*, in 8 NUOVO DIGESTO ITALIANO 1049 (Torino, UTET, 1939). *Cf.* V. EHRENBERG, 1 DER STAAT DER GRIECHEN 38, 42 f., 74 f. (Leipzig, Teubner, 1957).

[10] U.E. PAOLI, STUDI SUL PROCESSO ATTICO 55 (Padova, Cedam, 1933); P. DE FRANCISCI, 2 ARCANA IMPERII 100 (Milano, Giuffrè, 1948); C. HIGNETT, A HISTORY OF THE ATHENIAN CONSTITUTION TO THE END OF THE FIFTH CENTURY B.C. 299 ff. (Oxford, Clarendon Press, 1952); EHRENBERG, *supra* note 9, at 55, 75.

[11] PAOLI, *supra* note 10, at 23 ff., esp. at 27 ff.

not eventually ratified or, even if ratified, subsequently appeared inadvisable. Thus the power to change the laws was withdrawn from the whims of a majority in the popular Assembly (the *ecclesía*). This idea is also reflected in the philosophy of the greatest thinkers of that era. Plato, for example, believed the laws should reflect the divine order of things, being superior and not adaptable to the changing interests of men or classes of men. For Aristotle, the laws were norms above human passions,[12] and, significantly, he formulated a doctrine of the supremacy of the laws[13] and of the illegality of the unjust law.[14]

Nevertheless, the popular Assembly, or *ecclesía*, also had its own direct legislative power. [15] The decisions of the Assembly did not, however, assume either the form or the weight of *nómoi* but rather of *psephísmata*, which might be termed decrees. The *pséphisma* could deal with a wide range of matters; it could even consist of norms of general effect, binding on all the citizens. In such a case it was "assimilated" to the law.[16] One might also add that in certain of the more politically troubled times in the life of the Athenian *pólis*, the tendency to legislate by *psephísmata* became dominant. Nevertheless it remained a fundamental principle that the decree, whatever its content, had to be "legal both in form and in substance."[17] As modern jurists would say, it had to be *constitutional;* it could not be contrary to the existing *nómoi*.

The results of illegality (or, as we would say, of unconstitutionality) on the part of decrees emanating from the *ecclesía* were twofold. On the one hand there was a criminal liability incurred by the person who had proposed the decree; this liability gave rise to a public action called *graphè paranómon*, which had to be brought within one year. On the other hand, it seems that a decree contrary to a law was invalid following the principle—mentioned by Demosthenes—that the *nómos* was to prevail over a contrary *pséphisma*. [18] The Athenian judges, who were bound to adjudicate

---

[12] *Id.* at 29.

[13] *See* Passerin d'Entrèves, *Legalità e legittimità*, in 2 STUDI IN ONORE DI EMILIO CROSA 1309 (Milano, Giuffrè, 1960).

[14] CORWIN, *supra* note 8, at 7.

[15] EHRENBERG, *supra* note 9, at 42; PAOLI, *supra* note 10, at 55 f.

[16] PAOLI, *supra* note 10, at 55 f. *See also* EHRENBERG, *supra* note 9, at 42; DE FRANCISCI, *supra* note 10, at 105, 115.

[17] PAOLI, *supra* note 10, at 56; DE FRANCISCI, *supra* note 10, at 115 f.; EHRENBERG, *supra* note 9, at 42 f., 55.

[18] DE FRANCISCI, *supra* note 10, at 104, 116. *See also* BATTAGLINI, *supra* note 8, at 8-10.

"katà toùs nómous kaì katà psephísmata" (according to the laws and the decrees), were only bound to follow the *psephísmata* insofar as they were not in conflict with the *nómoi.*

This Greek distinction between ephemeral, man-made rules and the unchanging precepts of the "universal," "natural," or "divine" law has become a permanent feature of western thought. Sophocles, Plato, Aristotle, the Stoic philosophers, Cicero, and Roman jurisprudence as a whole with its distinction between the *jus gentium* and the *jus civile,* all tended to promote the idea of "one eternal and unchangeable law binding all nations through all time. . ."[19]

§ 3.   "Higher law" conceptions in medieval thought

Through Augustine, Isidore of Seville, Gratian and others,[20] Greco-Roman conceptions of higher law assumed a prominent position in the thought of the Middle Ages, though such conceptions, to be sure, were given considerable theological content. In the writings of Thomas Aquinas, for example, natural law was conceived as a *lex superior* of divine origins to which all other norms were subjected. As one modern jurist writes, "the act of the sovereign which violated the limits placed by natural law was declared null and void. The judge, whose job it was to apply the law, was bound to consider as void (and therefore not binding) both administrative acts and laws contrary to [natural] law, even if they emanated from the Pope or the Emperor. According to some theories, even individual subjects were freed from the duty to obey, when faced with a commandment which did not conform with the [natural] law, to such an extent that the forceful imposition of an unjust law justified armed resistance and even tyrannicide."[21] In place of the Roman or pseudo-Roman tenet that the sovereign

---

[19] From Cicero's *De Republica,* as quoted by CORWIN, *supra* note 8, at 10. *See also, e.g.,* B.F. BROWN, THE NATURAL LAW READER 47 (New York, Oceana Publications, 1960); G. Fassò, under *Giusnaturalismo,* in 7 NOVISSIMO DIGESTO ITALIANO 1106 (Torino, UTET, 1961); H. COING, NATURRECHT ALS WISSEN-SCHAFTLICHES PROBLEM 6 (Wiesbaden, Steiner Verlag, 1965). CORWIN, *supra* note 8, at 9-17, quotes several passages from Cicero as genuine "anticipations of judicial review."

[20] CORWIN, *supra* note 8, at 18.

[21] BATTAGLINI, *supra* note 8, at 13. The most thorough account of what has been mentioned in the text can be found in the famous works of O. VON GIERKE, JOHANNES ALTHUSIUS UND DIE ENTWICKLUNG DER NATURRECHTLICHEN STAATSTHEORIEN 272 f. *et passim* (Breslau, Koebner, 1880) and LES THÉORIES POLITIQUES DU MOYEN AGE 160-63 (J. de Pange, trans., Paris, Sirey, 1914). *See also* CORWIN, *supra* note 8, at 19 f.

is *not* subject to the laws *(Princeps legibus solutus)* some wished to substitute the opposite one: *Princeps legibus tenetur;* while others formulated a more moderate theory according to which the sovereign was not bound by civil law but was, however, bound by natural law.[22]

Medieval theories, therefore, clearly distinguished between two types of norm: that of the *jus naturale*, which was superior and inviolable, and that of the *jus positivum*, which was bound to conform with the former. The same distinction, for that matter, was drawn by the theories of the natural law school of the 17th and 18th centuries, from the time of Grotius up to Rousseau. Although its secular and rational basis brought it into opposition with medieval thought,[23] the natural law school of the 17th and 18th centuries affirmed the existence of "innate rights," intangible and inviolable, and, therefore, the existence of limitations and precepts binding on the legislator himself. This conception was so deeply rooted in the thought of that time that it is to be found even in the writings of the great theoretician of the English "Glorious Revolution" of 1688. John Locke, although asserting the absolute supremacy of Parliament—which, it has been said, "can do anything except transform a man into a woman and a woman into a man"—[24] admitted that the legislative power could be limited by natural law.[25]

It is true that this distinction between a natural law and a positive law was more suitable for exposition on a purely philosophical and theoretical level, separated from the facts of everyday life, than on the level of actual legal practice.[26] What, it may be asked, was the actual position of the judge faced with an unjust law? What

---

[22] BATTAGLINI, *supra* note 8, at 14.

[23] *See, e.g.,* Fassò, *supra* note 19, at 1106-08.

[24] On the questionable paternity of this phrase (De Lolme or Bagehot?) see W. HOLDSWORTH, 12 A HISTORY OF ENGLISH LAW 344 n.5 (London, Methuen, 1938, reprinted 1966); H.J. ABRAHAM, THE JUDICIAL PROCESS 295 (Oxford University Press, 2d ed. 1968). Even Blackstone in his *Commentaries* had asserted "that the power of Parliament is absolute and without control," see CORWIN, *supra* note 8, at 86 f., and that "to set the judicial power above that of the legislature . . . would be subversive of all government," see Plucknett, *Bonham's Case and Judicial Review,* 40 HARV. L. REV. 30, 59 f. (1926).

[25] *See* CORWIN, *supra* note 8, at 67 ff.; M. EINAUDI, LE ORIGINI DOTTRINALI E STORICHE DEL CONTROLLO GIUDIZIARIO SULLA COSTITUZIONALITÀ DELLE LEGGI NEGLI STATI UNITI D'AMERICA 20 ("Memorie dell'Istituto giuridico dell'Università di Torino," 1931); Cotta, *Montesquieu, la séparation des pouvoirs et la Constitution fédérale des Etats-Unis,* 1951 REVUE INTERNATIONALE D'HISTOIRE POLITIQUE ET CONSTITUTIONNELLE 229 f.

[26] *See* CORWIN, *supra* note 8, at 23.

was his position when faced with a law which he adjudged to conflict with a superior norm of natural law? The answer of the philosophers was clear. One might recall some especially famous passages of Thomas Aquinas in the *Summa Theologica* in which he affirms that the law contrary to natural law is void and has no binding force whatever.[27] However, despite such assertions from the philosophers, the fact remained that it was impossible to reconcile such theories with the realities of everyday life. On the one hand, there were the clear and precise rules of positive law, and on the other the imprecise and uncertain precepts of natural law. In effect, resolving a conflict between the two meant reconciling two distinct legal orders. A judge, faced with such a conflict, had to choose between applying the law of the state or the ill-defined principles of a legal system lacking both sanctions and institutions. Given this choice, it is not surprising that the judge would apply the positive law to concrete cases, leaving to the philosophers the airy formulations of natural law.

It was left to times nearer our own to provide the instruments whereby these two types of law could be assimilated within a unitary legal order. There was some divergence in the manner in which the natural law precepts evolved, were "positivized"[28] and absorbed into the sphere of positive law of various states. But a cursory glance at both French and English legal developments, for example, will show that the links between these early higher law theories and modern conceptions of judicial review are close indeed.

§ 4.   France: the Parlements and popular sovereignty

The French have clung tenaciously to the idea that no judicial organ should be given the power to review statutes for conformity

---

[27] *See, e.g.,* THOMAS AQUINAS, SUMMA THEOLOGICA II-II, *q.* 60, *art.* 5 ("Et ideo si scriptura legis contineat aliquid contra ius naturale, injusta est, nec habet vim obligandi . . . et ideo nec tales scripturae leges dicuntur, sed potius legis corruptiones . . . et ideo secundum eas non est judicandum"); *id.* I-II, *q.* 95, *art.* 2 ("Dicendum quod, sicut Augustinus dicit . . . non videtur esse lex, quae justa non fuerit. . . . Unde omnis lex humanitus posita intantum habet de ratione legis, in quantum a lege naturae derivatur. Si vero in aliquo a lege naturali discordet, iam non erit lex, sed legis corruptio"). *See* Passerin D'Entrèves, *Diritto naturale e distinzione fra morale e diritto nel pensiero di S. Tommaso d'Aquino,* 29 RIVISTA DI FILOSOFIA NEO-SCOLASTICA 3 f. (1937). *But see* G. FASSÒ, LA LEGGE DELLA RAGIONE 108 ff. (Bologna, Il Mulino, 2d ed. 1966).

[28] *See* P. PIOVANI, GIUSNATURALISMO ED ETICA MODERNA 46 (Bari, Laterza, 1961).

with a higher law.[29] The Constitutions of the Year VIII (1799), 1852, 1946, and 1958 did admit the possibility of constitutional control of legislation, but until recently such control has been, at best, theoretical, and it has always been entrusted to specifically political bodies.[30]

This rejection of judicial review does not mean that France has been immune to the attractions of higher law theory. There were, in fact, attempts during the *Ancien Régime* to affirm certain "fundamental" precepts. The *Parlements*, the higher courts set up in various French cities, came to assert in their relations with the French sovereign a power and duty "to examine all laws and de-

---

[29] *See, e.g.,* N. ALCALÁ-ZAMORA Y CASTILLO, ENSAYOS DE DERECHO PROCESAL CIVIL, PENAL Y CONSTITUCIONAL 514 n.26 (Buenos Aires, Edición de la Revista de Jurisprudencia, 1944); C.-A. COLLIARD, LIBERTÉS PUBLIQUES 38 f. (Paris, Dalloz, 3d ed. 1968); H. GALLAND, LE CONTRÔLE JUDICIAIRE DE LA CONSTITUTIONNALITÉ DES LOIS AUX ETATS-UNIS 14 (Paris, Sirey, 1932); Eisenmann & Hamon, *La Juridiction Constitutionnelle en Droit Français (1875-1961)*, in MAX-PLANCK-INSTITUT FÜR AUSLÄNDISCHES ÖFFENTLICHES RECHT UND VÖLKERRECHT, VERFASSUNGSGERICHTSBARKEIT IN DER GEGENWART, LÄNDERBERICHTE UND RECHTSVERGLEICHUNG 238 f. (H. Mosler (ed.), Köln-Berlin, Heymanns, 1962); F. Pierandrei, under *Corte costituzionale*, in 10 ENCICLOPEDIA DEL DIRITTO 887 f. (Milano, Giuffrè, 1962); Engel, *Judicial Review and Political Preview of Legislation in Post-War France*, 6 INTER-AM. L. REV. 53, 65 ff. (1964); King, *Constitutionalism and the Judiciary in France*, 80 POL. SCI. Q. 62-87 (1965).

[30] On the lack of success of the first two attempts to provide for a political control of constitutionality, those of the Constitutions of 1799 and 1852, see COLLIARD, *supra* note 29, at 38, 139; EINAUDI, *supra* note 25, at 13 f.; Engelhardt, *Das richterliche Prüfungsrecht im modernen Verfassungsstaat*, 8 JAHRBUCH DES ÖFFENTLICHEN RECHTS DER GEGENWART 102 f. (1959). With reference to the Constitution of 1946 see in general, JEANNE LEMASURIER, LA CONSTITUTION DE 1946 ET LE CONTRÔLE JURIDICTIONNEL DU LÉGISLATEUR (Paris, Pichon et Durand-Auzias, 1954); Buerstedde, *"Le comité constitutionnel" der französischen Verfassung von 1946*, 7 JAHRBUCH DES ÖFFENTLICHEN RECHTS DER GEGENWART 167 ff. (1958); Eisenmann & Hamon, *supra* note 29, at 242 f.; Engel, *supra* note 29, at 53 ff.; Massart, *Il controllo di legittimità costituzionale nella nuova Costituzione francese*, in 2 STUDI IN MEMORIA DI L. MOSSA 603, 605-07 (Padova, Cedam, 1961); Engelhardt, *supra* at 103. According to COLLIARD, *supra* note 29, at 35, the system adopted by the French Constitution of 1946 "constituait . . . la caricature même d'un contrôle de constitutionnalité." On the post-1958 *Conseil Constitutionnel*, see Ch. I, § 2 *supra*.

Not all the constitutions inspired by the ideology of the French Revolution rejected the idea of *judicial* review. When the French armies caused the Republic of Naples to be proclaimed in 1799, a committee was appointed to draw up a Constitution for the new state. The resulting document followed, by and large, the lead of the French Constitution of 1793, but in one interesting particular it declined to imitate this example. Claiming that a legislature on the French model "could concentrate in itself all powers and become despotic," the committee recommended the establishment of a "Supreme Tribunal," or "corpo degli efori," a judicial body which would declare if a legislative act was unconstitutional and would recommend that the legislature abrogate it. Though the proposed Constitution was never adopted, its original approach to constitutional control remains noteworthy. A. AQUARONE, M. D'ADDIO & G. NEGRI, LE COSTITUZIONI ITALIANE 269 (Milano, Edizioni di Comunità, 1958); BATTAGLINI, *supra* note 8, at 69 ff.

crees which come before us to see that there is in them nothing contrary . . . to the fundamental laws of the realm."[31] Through the work of the French *Parlements,* a doctrine was formulated which had a great effect on Montesquieu[32] and which shows a striking similarity to modern ideas of judicial review. This was the theory of the "heureuse impuissance" of the king to violate the fundamental laws, the "happy powerlessness" of the sovereign legislator to issue what we would call today unconstitutional laws.

But even as the judges proclaimed this limit on the royal power, the monarchs attempted to provide a means of insuring the supremacy of their own will. A *demande en cassation,* challenging a decision by a *Parlement,* could be brought before the sovereign's *Conseil des Parties* which could in turn annul the decision found to have been reached in violation of royal ordinances.[33]

---

[31] Thus the *Parlement* of Paris, in 1718; *see* Cotta, *supra* note 25, at 234 f., who quotes 1 REMONTRANCES DU PARLEMENT DE PARIS AU XVIIIe SIÈCLE 88 (J. Flammermont & M. Tourneux (eds.), Paris, 1888). *See also* Derathé, *Les philosophes et le despotisme,* in UTOPIE ET INSTITUTIONS AU XVIIIe SIÈCLE, LE PRAGMATISME DES LUMIÈRES 72-75 (Paris-La Haye, Mouton, 1963). On the evolution of the *Parlements* in the 17th and 18th centuries and on their function as "gardiens des lois fondamentales," see also J. ELLUL, HISTOIRE DES INSTITUTIONS DE L'ÉPOQUE FRANQUE À LA RÉVOLUTION 402-05 (Paris, Presses Universitaires de France, 5th ed. 1967). But even earlier, from the 16th century, one sees the development in France of the theory of *leges imperii* which, although distinct from divine and natural law, yet, like these, were not subject to amendment either by the king or by the *Etats généraux. Cf.* A. LEMAIRE, LES LOIS FONDAMENTALES DE LA MONARCHIE FRANÇAISE D'APRÈS LES THÉORICIENS DE L'ANCIEN RÉGIME 71-150 (Paris, A. Fontemoing, 1907); R.H. GIESEY, THE JURISTIC BASES OF DYNASTIC RIGHT TO THE FRENCH THRONE (Philadelphia, American Philosophical Society, 1961); extremely interesting is the passage from the TRAICTÉ DES SEIGNEURIES (1608) of Charles Loyseau reported by Mastellone, *Introduzione al pensiero politico di Charles Loyseau,* 4 CRITICA STORICA 448 (1965) ("La Souveraineté consiste en puissance absolue, c'est à dire parfaicte et entière de tout point. . . . Et comme la couronne ne peut être si son cercle n'est entier, aussi la souveraineté n'est point, si quelque chose y défaut. . . . Toutefois, comme il n'y a que Dieu qui soit tout puissant et que la puissance des hommes ne peut être absolue tout à fait, il y a trois sortes de lois qui bornent la puissance du Souverain, sans intéresser la Souveraineté. A savoir les lois de Dieu, pour ce que le Prince n'est pas moins souverain pour être sujet à Dieu; les règles de justice naturelles et non positives, parce que c'est le propre de la seigneurie publique d'être exercée par justice et non pas à discrétion: et finalement les lois fondamentales de l'Etat pour ce que le Prince doit user de sa Souveraineté selon sa propre nature et en la forme et aux conditions qu'elle est établie").
Even in other parts of Europe local courts attempted, from time to time, to assert a power of control similar to that of the French *Parlements. See* von Weber, *Schöppenstuhl und Landesherr. Ein Beitrag zur Geschichte der richterlichen Prüfungszuständigkeit,* in FESTSCHRIFT RICHARD THOMA 257 ff. (Tübingen, Mohr, 1950); Engelhardt, *supra* note 30, at 102.

[32] *See* Cotta, *supra* note 25, *passim,* esp. at 235 with reference to R. BICKART, LES PARLEMENTS ET LA NOTION DE SOUVERAINETÉ NATIONALE AU XVIIIe SIÈCLE 33 (Paris, Alcan, 1932).

[33] *See* P. CALAMANDREI, 1 LA CASSAZIONE CIVILE 264 ff., 290 ff., 313 ff., 355 ff. (Torino, Bocca, 1920); E. GLASSON & A. TISSIER, 1 TRAITÉ THÉORIQUE ET

Despite the existence of this check on the *parlementaires,* these judges of the higher courts acquired a reputation of interfering far too often with the activities of other state organs. Such interferences, though they might at times have been a salutary antidote to the absolutist tendencies of the monarchy,[34] more frequently smacked of an arbitrary abuse of power.[35] This was perhaps inherent in the attitude held by many judges toward their office. For them it was a "property right, a part of their estate," owned by them "by the same title they held their houses and lands."[36] As with their own property, "they bought and sold judgeships, transmitted them by bequest, and rented them out when they wished to hold them for their minor children."[37] Above all, they exploited their offices to the utmost—clearly at the expense of the litigants— just as a good landlord knows how best to exploit his lands. Not without reason were these judges almost always among the bitterest enemies of even the slightest liberal reform. They were the fiercest opponents of the Revolution, whose guillotine was soon to reap a rich harvest of their most honorable heads. Largely because of these abuses of the judicial function, the ideology of the Revolution, enshrined in the works of Rousseau and Montesquieu, stressed the omnipotence of statutory law, the equality of man before the law, and the rigid separation of powers in which the judge, the passive and "inanimate" *bouche de la loi,* performed the sole task of applying the letter of the law to individual cases—a task conceived as purely mechanical and in no way creative.

The legislature, therefore, as the voice of popular sovereignty, was seen as the best guarantor of fundamental rights. Concomitantly, and most significantly from the standpoint of the development of constitutional controls in continental Europe, there arose that "hostility which in France . . . has always been fostered against the notion that the acts of the superior organs and especially of the

---

PRATIQUE D'ORGANISATION JUDICIAIRE, DE COMPÉTENCE ET DE PROCÉDURE CIVILE 253 ff. (Paris, Sirey, 3d ed. 1925); P. Calamandrei, under *Cassazione civile,* in 2 NUOVO DIGESTO ITALIANO 987 f. (Torino, UTET, 1937).

[34] Cappelletti & Adams, *Judicial Review of Legislation: European Antecedents and Adaptations,* 79 HARV. L. REV. 1207, 1210 (1966).

[35] *Cf.* Buerstedde, *supra* note 30, at 172 f., 187; Eisenmann & Hamon, *supra* note 29, at 238 f.

[36] *See* the references in G. CHIOVENDA, 1 ISTITUZIONI DI DIRITTO PROCESSUALE CIVILE 134 (Napoli, Jovene, 2d ed. 1935). *See also* P. CUCHE & J. VINCENT, PROCÉDURE CIVILE 138 (Paris, Dalloz, 13th ed. 1963); P. HERZOG, CIVIL PROCEDURE IN FRANCE 45 (The Hague, Nijhoff, 1967).

[37] Carré, quoted by CHIOVENDA, *supra* note 36, at 134 ("'ils les achetaient, les vendaient, les transmettaient par héritage, les louaient quand ils voulaient les conserver à des mineurs'").

parliamentary assemblies, as representatives of national sovereignty, might be subjected to control" by the judiciary.[38]

§ 5. England and her colonies

Like France—indeed a century before France—England stoutly upheld the idea of parliamentary supremacy, though for different reasons. While both countries were long exposed to higher law theories, the English judiciary, unlike the French *Parlements,* generally enjoyed the respect of all as a protector of individual liberties against the government.[39] These two traditions—a consciousness of principles superior even to statutory law, and a profound regard for the judiciary and for its independence—were inherited by the American colonists, who were to find them most useful in their own situation during the revolutionary period and thereafter.

Pollock affirms the influence of natural law theories, at the same time explaining the failure of the bench and bar to admit such influence: "It is not credible that a doctrine which pervaded all political speculation in Europe, and was assumed as a common ground of authority by the opposing champions of the Empire and the Papacy, should have been without influence among learned men in England. If it be asked why the sages of the Common Law did not expressly refer to the Law of Nature, the answer is that at no time after, at latest, the Papal interference in the English politics of the first half of the thirteenth century, was the citation of Roman canonical authority acceptable in our country, save so far as it was [strictly] necessary . . . . These considerations appear sufficient to explain why "it is not used among them that be learned in the laws of England to reason what thing is commanded or prohibited by the Law of Nature.' "[40]

Prior to the 17th century, therefore, the English judicial tradition had often tended to assign a subordinate role to the legislative function of King and Parliament,[41] holding that law was not created

---

[38] F. Pierandrei, under *Corte costituzionale,* in 10 ENCICLOPEDIA DEL DIRITTO 887 (Milano, Giuffrè, 1962). As an example see E. LAMBERT, LE GOUVERNEMENT DES JUGES ET LA LUTTE CONTRE LA LÉGISLATION SOCIALE AUX ETATS-UNIS (Paris, Giard, 1921). *See also* King, *supra* note 29, at 63.

[39] *See, e.g.,* R. POUND, THE DEVELOPMENT OF CONSTITUTIONAL GUARANTEES OF LIBERTY 16 (New Haven, Conn., Yale University Press, 1957, 4th printing 1963). At times, of course, the judiciary, even in common law countries, jeopardized the respect it generally enjoyed. Examples are the English Star Chamber and the American Supreme Court in the early 20th century. *See* L.B. BOUDIN, GOVERNMENT BY JUDICIARY (New York, Russell & Russell, 1932); R.H. JACKSON, THE STRUGGLE FOR JUDICIAL SUPREMACY (New York, Random House, 1941); LAMBERT, *supra* note 38.

[40] F. POLLOCK, THE EXPANSION OF THE COMMON LAW 112 f. (London, Stevens and Sons, 1904).

but ascertained or declared. Common Law was fundamental law, and, although it could be complemented by the legislator, it could not be violated by him; hence law was largely withdrawn from arbitrary interventions of King and Parliament. This was the tradition Coke inherited and used as a weapon in his struggle against the exercise of arbitrary power by King James I.[42] The King claimed to be endowed with reason equal to that of the judges, his "delegates," and consequently claimed to be able to exercise the judicial power personally. Coke, however, replied that only judges could exercise that power, for only they were learned in the difficult science of law "which requires long study and experience, before that a man can attain to the cognizance of it."[43] On the other hand, Coke affirmed "the traditional supremacy of the common law over the authority of Parliament."[44] "It appears in our books," stated Coke in the famous *Bonham's Case* of 1610, "that in many cases, the common law will controul acts of parliament, and sometimes adjudge them to be utterly void: for when an act of parliament is against common right and reason, or repugnant, or impossible to be performed, the common law will controul it and adjudge such act to be void."[45] Elsewhere Coke further asserted: "Fortescue and Littleton and all others agree that the law consists of three parts: first, common law; secondly, statute law; third, custom, which takes

---

[41] See, for example, a well-known passage of the DE LEGIBUS ET CONSUETUDINIBUS ANCLIAE of Bracton, reported in CORWIN, *supra* note 8, at 27 (note also at 39, 49 n.27). *See also* E.S. CORWIN, LIBERTY AGAINST GOVERNMENT, esp. Ch. II (Baton Rouge, Louisiana State University Press, 1948).

[42] See von Mehren, *The Judicial Conception of Legislation in Tudor England,* in INTERPRETATIONS OF MODERN LEGAL PHILOSOPHIES. ESSAYS IN HONOR OF ROSCOE POUND 751-66 (New York, Oxford University Press, 1947); Cotta, *supra* note 25, at 235. For a more recent analysis of Coke's thought see J.W. GOUGH, FUNDAMENTAL LAW IN ENGLISH CONSTITUTIONAL HISTORY 30-47 (Oxford, Clarendon Press, 1955, reprinted 1961) (it may be said, in general, that the tendency of many commentators, especially Americans, to see in Coke a forerunner of the principle of judicial review has been criticized by others, especially the English, who interpret the thought of Coke in a more restrictive fashion).

[43] See CORWIN, *supra* note 8, at 38 f.

[44] Cotta, *supra* note 25, at 235. *See generally* W. HOLDSWORTH, 5 A HISTORY OF ENGLISH LAW 430 ff. (London, Methuen, 3d ed. 1945, reprinted 1966).

[45] 8 Coke's Reports 118 a; 77 Eng. Rep. 652. For an excellent commentary on *Dr. Bonham's Case* see Plucknett, *supra* note 24, at 30-70.

Professor Thorne has suggested that Coke's statement does not show a receptivity to natural law ideas, but that his "argument is derived from the ordinary common law rules of statutory interpretation" that a "repugnant" statute could not be applied. However, Professor Thorne would admit that the "repugnancy" of the statute in *Bonham's Case* lay in its inconsistency with a common law principle rather than with itself. Thorne, *Dr. Bonham's Case,* 54 LAW Q. REV. 543, 549, 551 (1938). Thus Coke's statement reflected a belief that statutes could not contradict fundamental law, even if this belief stemmed more from English legal rules than from natural law ideas current on the Continent. R. BERGER, CONGRESS V. THE SUPREME COURT 350 (Cam-

away the common law. But the common law corrects, allows and disallows both statute law and custom, for if there be repugnancy in statute or unreasonableness in custom, the common law disallows and rejects it."[46]

But who ought to control and ascertain such "repugnancy or unreasonableness," and who ought to guarantee the supremacy of the common law against arbitrary decisions of the sovereign on the one hand and of Parliament on the other? This was the essential question, and Coke's answer, at this point in his life, was clear and precise: that control and that guarantee were the task of the judges. This was the function of the judges who, in the words of a modern scholar, "being the only authorized interpreters of that law which is independent of the legislator, constitute therefore . . . a truly independent power."[47] While the influence of Coke's doctrine in *Bonham's Case* is debatable, Coke unquestionably reflected the attitude of many common law judges. This attitude deified the common law and looked with a jaundiced eye on any statute in derogation of that law. While few denied that Parliament could change the law, most retained a residual feeling that the long established principles of the common law were in some way superior to statutory innovations. Hence, statutes were, if at all possible, construed so as to preserve "the previous policy of the law."[48] "By the reign of Elizabeth, . . . many lawyers . . . gloried in the liberty which the courts enjoyed in playing fast and loose with statutes."[49]

Though the Glorious Revolution of 1688 marked the triumph of legislative supremacy in England, the American colonies had nonetheless inherited both Coke's ideas regarding the subordination of Crown and Parliament to higher law and a judiciary accustomed to interpreting and at times ignoring legislative acts violating higher

---

bridge, Harvard University Press, 1969). And this view was shared by common law judges at the time; "it would have required considerable audacity to deny that the only ultimate, supreme authority lay in a law higher than any man-made ordinance." C.K. ALLEN, LAW IN THE MAKING 446 (Oxford, Clarendon Press, 7th ed. 1964).

[46] Rowles v. Mason, 2 Brownl. 198 (1612). See CORWIN, *supra* note 8, at 50 f.; Cotta, *supra* note 25, at 236.

[47] Cotta, *supra* note 25, at 236.

[48] "The general words of an Act are not to be so construed as to alter the previous policy of the law unless no sense or meaning can be applied to those words consistently with the intention of preserving the existing policy untouched." *Minet v. Leman* (1855) as quoted in A. HARDING, A SOCIAL HISTORY OF ENGLISH LAW 232 (Harmondsworth, Middlesex, Penguin Books, 1966).

[49] T.F.T. PLUCKNETT, A CONCISE HISTORY OF THE COMMON LAW 334 (Boston, Little, Brown, 5th ed. 1956).

principles.[50] This legacy proved useful. James Otis invoked *Bonham's Case* against the Writs of Assistance,[51] and when, after independence, various state legislatures attempted to abolish debt collection, debase the currency and otherwise trample upon previously inviolable rights, the Federalists were quick to see the relevance of defining fundamental law in a national constitution and of using the judiciary to enforce that law.[52]

Paradoxically, the "Glorious Revolution" not only did not hinder, but rather it spurred the development of the new doctrine of judicial review. Under English law every corporation from private companies to municipal corporations "is entitled to act only within the limits of its own charter or constitution."[53] From that principle, the conclusion is derived that every act that exceeds the authority conferred on the corporation is null and void and cannot be enforced by the courts.[54]

The English colonies, often founded as commercial enterprises, were managed under Crown charters.[55] These "charters" may be considered as the first constitutions of the colonies,[56] both because they had a binding effect on colonial legislation and also because they regulated the fundamental legal structure of the colonies themselves. Frequently these "constitutions" expressly provided that the colonies could pass their own laws only if these laws were "reasonable" and "not contrary to the laws of the Kingdom of England."[57] Such provisions clearly imply that the laws should not be contrary to the sovereign will of the English Parliament.[58] Thus it was by reason of this supremacy of the English law and Parlia-

---

[50] B.F. WRIGHT, THE GROWTH OF AMERICAN CONSTITUTIONAL LAW 12 (Boston, Houghton Mifflin, 1942, reprinted 1967); Dietze, *Judicial Review in Europe*, 55 MICH. L. REV. 539, 549 (1957). For the influence of Coke's doctrine in the American colonies see BERGER, *supra* note 45, at 23-28.

[51] *See* A.H. KELLY & W.A. HARBISON, THE AMERICAN CONSTITUTION, ITS ORIGINS AND DEVELOPMENT 66-68 (New York, Norton, 3d ed. 1963). " 'That acts of Parliament against natural equity are void. That acts against the fundamental principles of the British constitution are void.' These words embodied ideas long familiar to New England minds: the supremacy of natural law, the idea of a supreme constitution, the doctrine of natural rights, and the limited power of human government." *Id.* at 67.

[52] *Id.* at 99-109. Between 1787-1803 there were more than twenty voidings by state courts of various state statutes. *Id.* at 100.

[53] GRANT, *supra* note 1, at 29.

[54] *Id.*

[55] *Id.*

[56] "Imperially granted constitutions or charters," according to the definition by McWhinney, *Constitutional Review in the Commonwealth, in* MAX-PLANCK-INSTITUT, *supra* note 29, at 75, 78.

[57] GRANT, *supra* note 1, at 29 f. *See also* MARCIC, *supra* note 8, at 179.

[58] *See* E. McWHINNEY, JUDICIAL REVIEW 13 f., 57 f. (University of Toronto Press, 4th ed. 1969).

ment that in numerous cases[59] the Privy Council of the King held that the colonial laws could not stand if they were opposed to the colonial charters or to the laws of the Kingdom.[60]

For these reasons the principle of *parliamentary supremacy*—and hence the supremacy of *positive law*[61]—which was introduced in England following the "Glorious Revolution" of 1688, produced quite different results in America than in England. In England the result was to remove every control over the validity of legislation from the judges, despite the early successes of Lord Coke's doctrine. In America, on the contrary, the result was to empower the colonial judges to disregard local legislation not in conformity with the English law. Thus the apparent paradox has been explained: how the English principle of the uncontrolled supremacy of the legislature helped, rather than hindered, the formation in America of an opposite system. This explanation is confirmed by the experience of other ex-colonies, including Canada, Australia, and India, which likewise adopted judicial review upon attaining independence.[62]

---

[59] It has been reckoned that more than 600 colonial laws were invalidated by the Privy Council from 1696 to 1782. WAGNER, *supra* note 3, at 87. It is not clear, however, whether this figure includes all of the English colonies, or is limited to those which came to comprise the original thirteen states. It would seem that the former is the case. J.H. SMITH, in his valuable work, APPEALS TO THE PRIVY COUNCIL FROM THE AMERICAN PLANTATIONS 524 (New York, Columbia University Press, 1950), notes that the function of "legislative" review (unconnected with concrete cases) exercised by the Privy Council vastly overshadowed that of judicial review. He shows that only 234 *judicial* appeals were entered in the Register of the Privy Council for the period 1696-1783. *Id.* at 667 ff. Another author appears to confirm this, saying that between 1691-1775, 59 Massachusetts statutes were disallowed under the general royal power to refuse assent to colonial legislation. During the same period, the Privy Council, in exercising its *judicial* function as a court of appellate jurisdiction, reviewed the validity of colonial legislation "at least four times with respect to legislation in the American colonies," the first case being that of Winthrop v. Lechmere in 1727. B.L. STRAYER, JUDICIAL REVIEW OF LEGISLATION IN CANADA 12 f. (University of Toronto Press, 1968).

[60] *See, e.g.,* Winthrop v. Lechmere (1727), and Philips v. Savage (1737). STRAYER, *supra* note 59, at 12 ff.; GRANT, *supra* note 1, at 30; C.G. HAINES, THE AMERICAN DOCTRINE OF JUDICIAL SUPREMACY 50 (Berkeley, University of California Press, 2d ed. 1932). On the Privy Council as "Final Appellate Tribunal for the Overseas Empire" see McWHINNEY, *supra* note 58, at 13 f., 49-60.

[61] EINAUDI, *supra* note 25, at 21.

[62] *See* Davison, *The Constitutionality and Utility of Advisory Opinions,* 2 U. TORONTO L.J. 254, 255 (1937-38); McWHINNEY, *supra* note 58, at 13 f., 49-60; McWhinney, *supra* note 56, at 75 ff.; Kapur, *The Supreme Court of India,* 11 JAHRBUCH DES ÖFFENTLICHEN RECHTS DER GEGENWART 2 f., 8 and *passim* (1962).

According to McWhinney, *supra,* at 78: "So far as the Supreme Courts of the individual Commonwealth Countries exercise judicial review of the constitution in their own right as the final appellate tribunals for their own particular countries, they may be said to be the lineal successors of the Privy Council." Hence the Privy Council is the essential link in the paradoxical de-

When the English colonies in America proclaimed their independence in 1776, one of their first acts was to substitute for the old "charters" new constitutions consisting of the fundamental laws of the newly independent states. And, just as laws contrary to the "charters" and to the "laws of the Kingdom" had been considered null and void by the judges, so it is not surprising that laws contrary to the new constitutions of the independent states should also be held null and void in the same way.[63] Though there is controversy over the authenticity of a number of precedents in this line of cases, several of them seem to be well verified.[64]

It should be emphasized, therefore, that more than a century of American history and a strong line of precedents—to say nothing of contemporary writings[65]—stood behind Chief Justice Marshall in 1803 when, interpreting the somewhat confused terms of article VI, paragraph 2 of the Federal Constitution of 1789, he enunciated "the principle, supposed to be essential to all written Constitutions, that a law repugnant to the Constitution is void; and that courts, as well as other departments, are bound by that instrument."

§ 6. Conclusion: the evolution of "constitutional justice"

So it is that judicial review, though it may come in varying forms to different countries at different times, is the result of an evolutionary pattern common to much of the West, in both civil and common law countries. First there was a period of "natural justice," when the acts of crown and parliament alike were said to be sub-

---

velopment of judicial review in the ex-colonies. Note, however, the exception of South Africa, where "the virtual absence of judicial review as known in the United States" is lamented; Karis, *The Republic of South Africa*, 15 JAHRBUCH DES ÖFFENTLICHEN RECHTS DER GEGENWART 613 (1966); see Ch. III, note 7 *infra*.

[63] See EINAUDI, *supra* note 25, at 21 ff.; Engelhardt, *supra* note 30, at 103.

[64] *E.g.*, the *"Ten Pound Act"* case (N.H. 1786) and Bayard v. Singleton, 1 N.C. (1 Martin) 5 (1787) (1901 Reprint). On the authenticity of these cases see BERGER, *supra* note 45, at 38 f.; W.W. CROSSKEY, 2 POLITICS AND THE CONSTITUTION IN THE HISTORY OF THE UNITED STATES 969-73 (University of Chicago Press, 1953); Levy, *Judicial Review, History and Democracy: An Introduction*, in JUDICIAL REVIEW AND THE SUPREME COURT: SELECTED ESSAYS 10 (L.W. Levy (ed.), New York, Harper & Row, 1967). For early federal precedents see H.E. DEAN, JUDICIAL REVIEW AND DEMOCRACY 23 f. (New York, Random House, 1966); HAINES, *supra* note 60, at Ch. VII.

[65] One might cite in particular those of James Otis and John Adams. CORWIN, *supra* note 8, at 77 ff.; S. CATINELLA, LA CORTE SUPREMA FEDERALE NEL SISTEMA COSTITUZIONALE DEGLI STATI UNITI D'AMERICA 30 f., 162 and *passim* (Padova, Cedam, 1934). For an analysis of the—not only American—ideology behind Marshall's enunciation of the principle of judicial review see R.H. GROSSMANN, DIE STAATS- UND RECHTSIDEOLOGISCHEN GRUNDLAGEN DER VERFASSUNGSGERICHTSBARKEIT IN DEN VEREINIGTEN STAATEN VON AMERIKA UND IN DER SCHWEIZ (Zürcher Dissert., Zürich, Schulthess, 1948).

ject to a higher, though unwritten, law. Then, with the "Glorious Revolution" in England and the French Revolution a century later, came the era of "positive" or "legal justice," characterized by the primacy of the written statute and the popular legislature, and the relative powerlessness of both judges and natural law theory to control this primacy.[66] This era carried a new flag to the citadel of justice: the "principle of legality." Institutions such as the "Cour de cassation" and the "Conseil d'Etat" were the instruments used to implement that principle.

Our own time has seen the burgeoning of "constitutional justice," which has in a sense combined the forms of legal justice and the substance of natural justice. Desirous of protecting the permanent will, rather than the temporary whims of the people,[67] many modern states have reasserted higher law principles through written constitutions. Thus there has been a synthesis of three separate concepts: the supremacy of certain higher principles, the need to put even the higher law in written form, and the employment of the judiciary as a tool for enforcing the constitution against ordinary legislation. This union of concepts first occurred in the United States, but it has since come to be considered by many as essential to the rule of law *(Rechtsstaat)* anywhere.

This does not mean that the periods which preceded that of constitutional justice were without rational foundation. The principle of legality certainly improved upon the version of natural law ideas used to justify the arbitrariness of such previous courts as the French *Parlements;* yet legality itself proved subject to perversion during the twentieth century. Modern constitutionalism is a sort

---

[66] For an illustration of the downgrading of natural law theories during the 19th and early part of the 20th century see the comments of the German jurist J. Kohler, *Rechtsphilosophie und Universalrechtsgeschichte*, in 1 Enzyklopädie der Rechtswissenschaft Holtzendorff-Kohler 3 f. (München-Leipzig, Duncker & Humblot, 7th ed. 1915); *see* Coing, *supra* note 19, at 8, 13 ff.

[67] ". . . where the will of the legislature, declared in its statutes, stands in opposition to that of the people, declared in the Constitution, the judges ought to be governed by the latter rather than the former." The Federalist No. 78 (Hamilton). *See* Einaudi, *supra* note 25, at 9; Kadish, *Judicial Review in the United States Supreme Court and the High Court of Australia*, 37 Texas L. Rev. 1, 8 (1958).

of Hegelian synthesis which attempts to apply the lessons, while avioding the pitfalls, of the past.[68]

---

[68] It has been said that "the civil and political liberties upon which the modern State is founded are triumphs of natural law" (Fassò, *supra* note 19, at 1108); and that "the problem of natural rights can today only be confronted on the level of constitutionalism" (Matteucci, *Positivismo giuridico e costituzionalismo,* 17 RIVISTA TRIMESTRALE DI DIRITTO E PROCEDURA CIVILE 988 (1963)).

For an analysis of the evolution of both civil and common law worlds from "natural justice" through "legal justice" to "constitutional justice" see Cappelletti, *The Significance of Judicial Review of Legislation in the Contemporary World,* in 1 JUS PRIVATUM GENTIUM. FESTSCHRIFT FÜR MAX RHEINSTEIN ZUM 70. GEBURTSTAG AM 5. JULI 1969, at 147, 155-59 (Tübingen, Mohr, 1969).

CHAPTER III

THE MODERN SYSTEMS OF JUDICIAL REVIEW: THE ORGANS OF CONTROL

§ 1. Introduction

Though the events of the 20th century brought the West as a whole to see the value of judicial review of the constitutionality of legislation, the historical and philosophical differences between the states of the West prevented their adopting identical systems of such control. Deep-seated suspicions of the judicial office, commitments to legal positivism, and other more practical considerations have meant that judicial review in various countries is conducted by different *organs* of review, which employ different *methods,* and whose decisions may have differing *effects.* It is this array of organs, methods, and effects which will be discussed here and in succeeding chapters.[1]

---

[1] Clearly it will not be possible to make a sort of universal encyclopedia, and this study makes no claim to completeness. For example, one institution which we have intentionally omitted from our analysis despite its interesting origins is the Brazilian *mandado de segurança.* Also, we have given only a summary treatment to the Mexican (and no longer only Mexican) *juicio de amparo.* See the interesting study of Buzaid, *"Juicio de Amparo" e Mandado de Segurança (Contrastes e confrontes),* 3 REVISTA DE DIREITO PROCESSUAL CIVIL 30-70 (1962) (on the problem of the admissibility of *mandado de segurança* even against legislative acts see esp. 65 f.). In fact, the largest gap in this comparative study is the omission of the Latin American countries, several of which have some kind of judicial review. For information on this subject see J.A.C. GRANT, EL CONTROL JURISDICCIONAL DE LA CONSTITUCIONALIDAD DE LAS LEYES. UNA CONTRIBUCIÓN DE LAS AMÉRICAS A LA CIENCIA POLÍTICA 73 ff. (Publicación de la Facultad de Derecho de México, 1963); E. VESCOVI, EL PROCESO DE INCONSTITUCIONALIDAD DE LA LEY 27 ff. and *passim* (Montevideo, Facultad de Derecho y Ciencias Sociales, 1967); H. FIX ZAMUDIO, VEINTICINCO AÑOS DE EVOLUCIÓN DE LA JUSTICIA CONSTITUCIONAL 1940-1965, esp. at 25 ff. (México, UNAM—Instituto de Investigaciones Jurídicas, 1968); C.A. LÚCIO BITTENCOURT, O CONTRÔLE JURISDICIONAL DA CONSTITUCIONALIDADE DAS LEIS (Rio, Forense, 2d ed. 1968).
  Also omitted is a discussion of judicial review in certain of the newly emergent African and Asian states, though the adoption of this institution by non-western cultures is of deep significance and is certainly deserving of separate study. See, for examples, J. BUCHMANN, L'AFRIQUE NOIRE INDEPENDANTE 184 ff. (Paris, Pichon et Durand-Auzias, n.d.); P. CONTINI, THE SOMALI REPUBLIC: AN EXPERIMENT IN LEGAL INTEGRATION 40-42 (London, Cass, 1969); FIX ZAMUDIO, *supra* at 51-63, 90-99.

§ 2. Judicial review: centralized or decentralized

One might distinguish two broad types of judicial control over the constitutionality of legislation:[2]

a) The "decentralized" type gives the power of control to *all the judicial organs* of a given legal system. This has also been called the "American" system of control.[3] Indeed, we have seen in Chapter II that in one sense the beginnings of this type of control may be found in the United States, where judicial review remains the most characteristic and "unique" institution.[4]

b) The "centralized" type of control confines the power of review to *one single judicial organ*.[5] By analogy, the "centralized" type might be referred to as "Austrian," for the archetype is contained in the Austrian Constitution of October 1, 1920 (the so-called *Oktoberverfassung*). This Constitution, based on proposals

---

[2] Alternative terminology would call the systems "diffuse" and "concentrated." P. Calamandrei, La illegittimità costituzionale delle leggi 5 (Padova, Cedam, 1950), republished in 3 Opere giuridiche 349 (M. Cappelletti (ed.), Napoli, Morano, 1968). In German terminology one talks of an *allgemeines Prüfungsrecht* (or *allgemeine Normenkontrolle*) and of a *konzentriertes Prüfungsrecht* (or *konzentrierte Normenkontrolle*); see, for example, Engelhardt, *Das richterliche Prüfungsrecht im modernen Verfassungsstaat*, 8 Jahrbuch des öffentlichen Rechts der Gegenwart 107 f. (1959).

[3] See, e.g., H. Fix Zamudio, El Juicio de Amparo 379 n.33 (México, Porrúa, 1964).

[4] B.F. Wright, The Growth of American Constitutional Law 5 (Boston, Houghton Mifflin, 1942, reprinted 1967); M. Shapiro, Law and Politics in the Supreme Court 3 (London, Collier-Macmillan, 1964).

[5] There are also what might be called "mixed" or "intermediate" systems: e.g., in Mexico, where because of a prima facie divergence between articles 103 and 133 of the Constitution, it would be difficult to put the system into one or the other of the categories given in the text (see also for other references Fix Zamudio, *supra* note 3, at 167-94, 246-57, 296-98, 378-80, and esp. 175-80, 247-51). This is true not only from the point of view of the *organs* of control, but also from that of the *method* by which questions of constitutional legitimacy are resolved. Even in the latter respect the Mexican system has a place somewhere between the systems working "by way of direct action" and those working "by way of defense" (see Ch. IV, especially note 21, *infra*). Another mixed system is the Irish one. See generally J.M. Kelly, Fundamental Rights in the Irish Law and Constitution 15-36 (New York, Oceana, 2d ed. 1968); Azzariti, *I vari sistemi di sindacato sulla costituzionalità delle leggi nei diversi paesi*, in La Corte costituzionale (raccolta di studi) 35 f. (supplement of La Rassegna mensile dell'Avvocatura dello Stato, Roma, Istituto poligrafico dello Stato, 1957).
Particularly complex, and as yet unclear, is the system of judicial review vaguely affirmed for the first time by the Israeli Supreme Court in its decision of July 3, 1969. See Klein, *Les problèmes constitutionnels de l'Etat d'Israël et le contrôle de la constitutionnalité des lois*, 85 Revue du droit public et de la science politique en France et à l'étranger 1105 ff., 1117 ff., esp. 1122-24 (1969); Nimmer, *The Uses of Judicial Review in Israel's Quest for a Constitution*, 70 Colum. L. Rev. 1217 (1970).

formulated by the Austrian jurist Hans Kelsen, was re-enacted in Austria after World War II, as amended by the *Novelle* of 1929.[6]

Both of these systems have been introduced, even very recently, in several countries, and thus have served as models outside their country of origin.

The "American," or North American, system of judicial review is found primarily in many of Britain's former colonies, including Canada, Australia, and India.[7] In the previous chapter we tried to

---

[6] See the *Verfassungsüberleitungsgesetz* of May 1, 1945.

[7] See J. BROSSARD, LA COUR SUPRÊME ET LA CONSTITUTION. LE FORUM CONSTITUTIONNEL AU CANADA 66 ff., 73 ff. (Montréal, Les Presses de l'Université de Montréal, 1968); E. McWHINNEY, JUDICIAL REVIEW (University of Toronto Press, 4th ed. 1969); McWhinney, *Constitutional Review in the Commonwealth*, in MAX-PLANCK-INSTITUT FÜR AUSLÄNDISCHES ÖFFENTLICHES RECHT UND VÖLKERRECHT, VERFASSUNGSGERICHTSBARKEIT IN DER GEGENWART. LÄNDERBERICHTE UND RECHTSVERGLEICHUNG 75 ff. (H. Mosler (ed.), Köln-Berlin, Heymanns, 1962); Economou, *Le Contrôle juridictionnel de la Constitutionnalité des lois dans les Pays de Droit Commun*, 11 REVUE HELLÉNIQUE DE DROIT INTERNATIONAL 336 ff. (1958); Engelhardt, *supra* note 2, at 105, 110; Kadish, *Judicial Review in the United States Supreme Court and the High Court of Australia*, 37 TEXAS L. REV. 1 (1958). The statement in the text may need qualification as regards India. M. AMAM, THE INDIAN SUPREME COURT AND THE CONSTITUTION: A STUDY OF THE PROCESS OF CONSTRUCTION 18 (Delhi, East Book Co., 1968); Geck, *Judicial Review of Statutes: A Comparative Survey of Present Institutions and Practices*, 51 CORNELL L.Q. 250, 256 (1966).

Engelhardt indicates at 110 that in Canada (and to some extent in Australia) the system adopted is as follows: the question of the validity of a law, having been raised as a preliminary issue in a civil case either by one of the parties or by the judge on his own motion, must always be referred by the inferior court to the Supreme Court, which therefore has a sort of monopoly over constitutional interpretation. From this premise Engelhardt comes to a much wider conclusion, namely that the trend is either to entrust judicial review to one special organ, or, at least, to confine it to *one* of the ordinary courts. However, the premise seems to be only partly correct. In reality the current Canadian system is substantially "identical to that of the United States" (Grant, *Judicial Review in Canada: Procedural Aspects*, 42 CAN. B. REV. 195 ff., esp. 197 f. (1964); GRANT, *supra* note 1, at 86 ff.). *See also* BROSSARD, *supra* at 140 f., 143, 150-52; Russell, *The Jurisdiction of the Supreme Court of Canada: Present Policies and a Programme for Reform*, 6 OSGOODE HALL L.J. 1, 7 f. (1968). The same can be said, to a large extent, for the systems adopted by other countries in the Commonwealth (see Ch. II, text and notes 62-64 *supra*). Nevertheless, it is true that in Canada there exist, alongside the normal (decentralized) method of judicial review, certain "special procedures to litigate constitutional issues" (Grant, *supra* at 200 ff.). One of these, which has been adopted in six of the ten Canadian Provinces, is the possibility of bringing the question of constitutionality before the Supreme Court *per saltum* by suspending the case in which it has arisen. This procedure has the purpose of obtaining a speedy and unchallengeable decision upon the preliminary issue, which would anyway, in the last instance, have come before the Supreme Court. One writer has said, however, that he knows "of no cases which have actually reached the Supreme Court through the use of this machinery." Russell, *supra* at 8 n.20. *See also* B. LASKIN, CANADIAN CONSTITUTIONAL LAW 151 (Toronto, Carswell, 3d ed. 1966); BROSSARD, *supra* at 142 f.

In South Africa, judicial review was, for practical purposes, abolished in 1961. This has been seen as an effort to counter the Supreme Court's opposition to policies of racial discrimination in that country. *See* FIX ZAMUDIO, *supra* note 1, at 60 f.; Ch. II, note 62 *supra*.

explain the apparent paradox which led to the establishment of judicial review in the colonies, despite its rejection in England where the principle of parliamentary supremacy prevailed.

The American system of control has also been introduced in Japan under the current Japanese Constitution of May 3, 1947.[8] In Europe as well, the American system has had and still has its analogues. A certain parallel can be found, for example, in Swiss law, where, alongside a direct action before the Federal Tribunal *(staatsrechtliche Beschwerde* or *recours de droit public)*, there exists a general right of review *(richterliches Prüfungsrecht)* in the ordinary courts. Although this judicial review is limited to the laws of the cantons and has much less practical importance than the direct action just mentioned, the Swiss judges have a general power to disregard laws of the cantons in conflict with the Federal Constitution. This power has been derived from the principle that federal law "breaks" cantonal law *(Bundesrecht bricht kantonales Recht)*. However, there is no judicial control over the constitutionality of federal laws; this limitation has been criticized by modern writers, although it is a traditional feature of the Swiss legal system.[9]

---

[8] *See* Kiyomiya, *Verfassungsgerichtsbarkeit in Japan,* in MAX-PLANCK-INSTI-TUT, *supra* note 7, at 328, 336; Hayashida, *Constitutional Court and Supreme Court of Japan,* in 2 DIE MODERNE DEMOKRATIE UND IHR RECHT. FESTSCHRIFT FÜR GERHARD LEIBHOLZ ZUM 65. GEBURTSTAG 422 f. (Tübingen, Mohr, 1966). Upon the curious origins of the Japanese Constitution of 1947, which was half-way between an imposition and an imitation of American ideas, see Abe, *Die Entwicklung des japanischen Verfassungsrechts seit 1952,* 15 JAHRBUCH DES ÖFFENTLICHEN RECHTS DER GEGENWART 516 (1966); Nathanson, *Constitutional Adjudication in Japan,* 7 AM. J. COMP. L. 195, 217 (1958).

Note also that though the Japanese Supreme Court in 1952 conclusively decided to entertain constitutional cases in accordance with the "decentralized" American pattern, there had been some previous academic opinions advanced that the Japanese high court ought to hear constitutional cases in the abstract while sitting as a special constitutional court. FIX ZAMUDIO, *supra* note 1, at 53; Henderson, *Introduction, Symposium on the Japanese Constitution,* 43 WASH. L. REV. 887, 1009 ff. (1968).

[9] On the *staatsrechtliche Beschwerde* or *recours de droit public,* which can be brought, within a short time limit, against legislative enactments of the cantons which contravene provisions enshrined in the Constitution see M. CAPPELLETTI, LA GIURISDIZIONE COSTITUZIONALE DELLE LIBERTÀ 23-35 (Milano, Giuffrè, 1955); Z. GIACOMETTI, DIE VERFASSUNGSGERICHTSBARKEIT DES SCHWEIZERISCHEN BUNDESGERICHTES (DIE STAATSRECHTLICHE BESCHWERDE) (Zürich, Polygraphischer Verlag, 1933); J. ROUSSY, LE CONTRÔLE JUDICIAIRE DE LA CONSTITUTIONNALITÉ DES LOIS FÉDÉRALES AUX ETATS-UNIS ET EN SUISSE 128 ff. (Lausanne, Editions Thonney-Dupraz, 1969); Imboden, *Verfassungsge-richtsbarkeit in der Schweiz,* in MAX-PLANCK-INSTITUT, *supra* note 7, at 510 f., 515 ff. See Ch. I, § 8c *supra.*

For the general power-duty of all Swiss courts (and not only the Federal Tribunal) not to apply cantonal laws conflicting with the Constitution, even if the time limit for the *staatsrechtliche Beschwerde* may have elapsed, see Imboden, *supra* at 507, 511 ff., esp. 513; *see also* ROUSSY, *supra* at 126, 155. On the inadmissibility of any type of judicial control of federal laws see A. FAVRE, DROIT CONSTITUTIONNEL SUISSE 427 ff. (Fribourg, Editions universi-

Norwegian law (since the end of the last century) and Danish law (from the beginning of this century) have also asserted the "incontestable" power of the courts to review the conformity of legislation with the constitution and to disregard, in the concrete case, a law held unconstitutional, although admittedly this power has been used with extreme moderation and fairly infrequently.[10] A similar power has also been asserted in Sweden in the last few years.[11]

Germany and Italy, where today we find the centralized rather than the decentralized system, also experimented briefly with the American type of control: Germany under the Weimar Constitution[12] and Italy from 1948 to 1956, that is to say from the adoption

---

taires, 1966); R.H. Grossmann, Die staats- und rechtsideologischen Grundlagen der Verfassungsgerichtsbarkeit in den Vereinigten Staaten von Amerika und in der Schweiz 3 f. (Zürcher Dissertation, Zürich, Schulthess, 1948); Imboden, *supra* at 513 f.; Schindler, Jr., *Richterliches Prüfungsrecht und politischer Mehrheitswille, Erfahrungen der Vereinigten Staaten —Folgerungen für die Schweiz*, 74 Zeitschrift für schweizerisches Recht 289 f., 312 f. (1955). For an account of current criticisms of this exclusion, which are largely inspired by the United States system, see E. Wolf, Verfassungsgerichtsbarkeit und Verfassungstreue in den Vereinigten Staaten 1-4, 230-37 (Basel, Helbing & Lichtenhahn, 1961), who is in opposition to the critics.

[10] *See generally* F. Castberg, Die Zuständigkeit der Gerichte in USA und Norwegen zur Prüfung der Verfassungsmässigkeit von Gesetzen (Karlsruhe, Müller, 1960); Castberg, *Verfassungsgerichtsbarkeit in Norwegen und Dänemark*, in Max-Planck-Institut, *supra* note 7, at 418-21, 428; Engelhardt, *supra* note 2, at 104. For further information on the Norwegian system see Cappelletti & Adams, *Judicial Review of Legislation: European Antecedents and Adaptations*, 79 Harv. L. Rev. 1207, 1217 (1966).

[11] Up to 1964, despite some academic opinions to the contrary, it was held in Sweden, as opposed to Norway and Denmark, that the judges did not have the power of judicial review of legislation. Ruth B. Ginsburg & A. Bruzelius, Civil Procedure in Sweden 10, 131 (The Hague, Nijhoff, 1965); Herlitz, *Verfassungsgerichtsbarkeit in Schweden*, in Max-Planck-Institut, *supra* note 7, at 494-97. This view was, however, upset by the noteworthy decision of the Swedish Supreme Court on November 13, 1964 (published in 1964 Nytt Juridiskt Arkiv 471 and in 1965 Nordisk Domssamling 429). On this see the discussion of G. Petrén in 1966 Svensk Juristtidning 432.

As for another Scandinavian country, Finland, it is still the rule that no judicial review of legislation is allowed. Kastari, *Verfassungsgerichtsbarkeit in Finnland*, in Max-Planck-Institut, *supra* note 7, at 215-17; Merikoski, *The System of Government*, in The Finnish Legal System 39 f. (J. Uotila (ed.), Helsinki, The Union of Finnish Lawyers Publishing, 1966); Saario, *Control of the Constitutionality of Laws in Finland*, 12 Am. J. Comp. L. 194 ff., 203-05 (1963). This rule has not, however, failed to provoke considerable discussion in Finnish academic circles. See the references in *id.* at 203-05 nn.32, 34 and 35. On the Finnish Constitutional Committee see Ch. I, note 28 *supra*.

[21] *See*, for example, W. Apelt, Geschichte der Weimarer Verfassung 286-89 (München-Berlin, Beck, 2d ed. 1964); C.J. Friedrich, The Impact of American Constitutionalism Abroad 82 (Boston University Press, 1967); H. Spanner, Die richterliche Prüfung von Gesetzen und Verordnungen 5 (Wien, Springer Verlag, 1951) ("Die Praxis der Gerichte hat sich nach der grundsätzlichen Entscheidung des Reichsgerichts vom 4. November 1925 . . . allgemein zur Bejahung des richterlichen Prüfungsrechts gegenüber Gesetzen bekannt, und zwar zu einem *Prüfungsrecht, das jedem Gericht zusteht*, wenn die

of the "rigid" Constitution until the Constitutional Court began to function.[13]

But however widespread has been the acceptance of the older, decentralized system of control of constitutionality, also remarkable has been the expansion, especially in recent years, of the centralized or Austrian system. Unsuccessful attempts were made to adopt it in Czechoslovakia in 1920[14] and in Spain in 1931,[15] but they were not very significant largely due to the short and stormy lives of these two Republics.[16] The centralized system was adopted by the Constitution of the Italian Republic of January 1, 1948 and by the Bonn Constitution of May 23, 1949, both still in force.[17] This system was also established by the Constitution of the Republic of

---

Frage der Verfassungsmässigkeit eines Gesetzes eine Vorfrage für die vom Gericht zu treffende Entscheidung bildet. Das Gericht ist . . . nur befugt, dem für verfassungswidrig erachteten Gesetz im konkreten Fall die Anwendung zu versagen"); Engelhardt, *supra* note 2, at 106; Friesenhahn, *Die Verfassungsgerichtsbarkeit in der Bundesrepublik Deutschland*, in MAX-PLANCK-INSTITUT, *supra* note 7, at 96 f.; Geck, *supra* note 7, at 254. Extensive information on the subject can be found in Dietze, *Judicial Review in Europe*, 55 MICH. L. REV. 539, 544 ff. (1957).

[13] This transition period (on which see art. VII, para. 2, of the "Disposizioni transitorie e finali" of the Constitution) was to last until the Constitutional Court, provided for by the Constitution, began to function in 1956.

Some other European precedents of decentralized control of the constitutionality of legislation are mentioned by S. CATINELLA, LA CORTE SUPREMA FEDERALE NEL SISTEMA COSTITUZIONALE DEGLI STATI UNITI D'AMERICA 111 ff., esp. at 115, 125 (Padova, Cedam, 1934); Deener, *Judicial Review in Modern Constitutional Systems*, 46 AM. POL. SCI. REV. 1083 (1952); Engelhardt, *supra* note 2, at 104 (but the lack of practical success of these precedents is well-known). The precedents are certain cases at the beginning of this century when Rumanian and Greek courts refused to apply unconstitutional laws, and also art. 63 of the Portuguese Constitution of 1911, which expressly gave the courts the power to disregard such laws. For further developments in these countries see Azzariti, *supra* note 5, at 20 (Rumania), 28 f. (Greece), 31 f. (Portugal); Deener, *supra* at 1087; Engelhardt, *supra* note 2, at 104.

Professor Lucas Prakke of the University of Amsterdam kindly informs me that a proposal for the introduction of a decentralized system of judicial review has been under serious consideration in Holland; it is included in the tentative text of a new Constitution published by the Ministry of the Interior and approved by an Advisory Committee on matters of constitutional and electoral law.

[14] This attempt was almost contemporary with that more fortunate one in neighboring Austria. See arts. 1-3 of the law of February 29, 1920, preliminary to the Constitution of the Czechoslovak Republic; art. 102 of the Czech Constitution of 1920; Azzariti, *supra* note 5, at 18, 41; Deener, *supra* note 13, at 1086; Engelhardt, *supra* note 2, at 105 f., 111 f., 115.

[15] See Alcalá-Zamora y Castillo, *Significado y funciones del Tribunal de Garantías Constitucionales*, in ENSAYOS DE DERECHO PROCESAL CIVIL, PENAL Y CONSTITUCIONAL 503 ff. (Buenos Aires, Edición de la Revista de Jurisprudencia Argentina, 1944); Azzariti, *supra* note 5, at 45.

[16] It seems that neither in Czechoslovakia nor in Spain did the Constitutional Courts ever have the opportunity of exercising their power of judicial review. Azzariti, *supra* note 5, at 45; Engelhardt, *supra* note 2, at 118.

[17] For Italy see arts. 134-137 of the Constitution; the constitutional laws of February 9, 1948, No. 1, and March 11, 1953, No. 1; and the ordinary law of March 11, 1953, No. 87. For Germany see arts. 93-94, 99-100 of the *Bon-*

Cyprus of August 16, 1960;[18] by the Constitution of the Turkish Republic of July 9, 1961;[19] and finally by the Constitution of the Federal Socialist Republic of Yugoslavia of April 7, 1963. This latter is the first and, up to now, the only Constitution of a country under a Communist regime to adopt a system of judicial review, though, significantly, a recent Czechoslovakian constitutional law has contemplated the establishment of constitutional courts, both on a federal and on a state level. In Yugoslavia, the review is exercised by a special Federal Constitutional Court and, on the regional level, by special Constitutional Courts in the six Federate Republics.[20]

---

ner Grundgesetz, and the ordinary law of March 12, 1951 on the *Bundesverfassungsgericht* and subsequent amendments.

[18] See Blümel, *Die Verfassungsgerichtsbarkeit in der Republik Zypern,* in MAX-PLANCK-INSTITUT, *supra* note 7, at 643 ff., 676 ff. (the English text of the Cypriot Constitution can be found in A.J. PEASLEE, 3 CONSTITUTIONS OF NATIONS (The Hague, Nijhoff, 3d ed. 1968)). *See also* Tzermias, *Die Verfassung der Republik Cypern,* 10 JAHRBUCH DES ÖFFENTLICHEN RECHTS DER GEGENWART 485 ff. (1961).

The Cypriot Constitution is *sui generis,* both because of the extraordinary efforts made to protect the rights of the Greek and the Turkish populations and because of the combination of continental and common law influences evident in the provisions concerning judicial review. Such review is concentrated, theoretically, in one Supreme Constitutional Court; initiative may be either by certain high officials or by parties involved in ordinary litigation. See Ch. V, note 14 *infra.*

Another sidelight is the fact that in 1964 an Administration of Justice Act was passed which, in light of the conflicts between the two major communities, temporarily joined the functions of the special Constitutional Court and the High Court (the court of last instance in ordinary litigation) in a single Supreme Court. *See* PEASLEE, *supra* at 137, 216. The consequences of this merger are far-reaching. Recent decisions by the new Supreme Court seem to transform the centralized system, clearly provided for by the Constitution, into a decentralized one, in which all courts may decide constitutional issues raised before them. *See* Attorney-General of the Republic v. Mustafa Abrahim, in 1964 CYPRUS LAW REPORTS 195 ff., esp. 205 f., 269-74.

[19] See Ülkü Azrak, *Verfassungsgerichtsbarkeit in der Türkei,* 11 JAHRBUCH DES ÖFFENTLICHEN RECHTS DER GEGENWART 73 ff. (1962); Abadan, *Die türkische Verfassung von 1961,* 13 *id.* (1964), at 325 ff., esp. 408 ff.; Bekir Balta, *Die Verfassungsgerichtsbarkeit in der Türkei,* in MAX-PLANCK-INSTITUT, *supra* note 7, at 550 ff. (an English translation of the Turkish Constitution can be found in PEASLEE, *supra* note 18).

[20] Arts. 100, 101 of the Constitutional Act No. 143 of 27 October 1968 of Czechoslovakia provided for a similar system. For a translation of the Act see Z. JICÍNSKY & J. SKÁLA, THE CZECHOSLOVAK FEDERATION (Prague, Orbis, 1969). The final implementing legislation has not yet been enacted, and under the present circumstances is not likely to be.

One cannot fail to notice that this new element in constitutional law profoundly transforms Communist theories of state and law. *See* J.-P. Ferretjans, *La Constitution du 7 avril 1963 de la République socialiste fédérative de Yougoslavie et l'unité marxiste du pouvoir d'état,* 79 REVUE DU DROIT PUBLIC ET DE LA SCIENCE POLITIQUE EN FRANCE ET À L'ÉTRANGER 939 ff., 948 ff. (1963); Kastari, *Le caractère normatif et la prééminence hiérarchique des Constitutions,* 18 REVUE INTERNATIONALE DE DROIT COMPARÉ 831, 845 f. (1966); *see generally* Djordjevic, *Les Cours constitutionnelles en Yougoslavie,* 14 (No. 4) LE NOUVEAU DROIT YOUGOSLAVE 9 ff. (1963); Krbek, *Die Verfassung der Sozia-*

§ 3. The rationale of the decentralized form of judicial review

The theory behind giving the entire judiciary the duty of constitutional control is, on its face, logical and simple, as is apparent from Marshall's judgment in *Marbury v. Madison* and earlier from the writings of Alexander Hamilton.[21]

Substantially, the argument is as follows:

a) The function of all judges is to interpret the laws, in order to apply them to the concrete cases which come before them.

b) One of the more obvious canons of interpretation of legislation is that when two legislative enactments conflict with each other, the judge must apply the prevailing one.

c) Given two enactments of equal normative force, the prevailing one will be determined by the traditional criteria of "lex posterior derogat legi priori," "lex specialis derogat legi generali," etc.

d) But, clearly, these criteria are no longer valid when the conflict is between enactments of different normative force. In this

---

listischen Föderativen Republik Jugoslawien vom 7.4.1963, 13 JAHRBUCH DES ÖFFENTLICHEN RECHTS DER GEGENWART 243 ff., esp. 267 f., 280 ff. (1964); Srzentic, *Sur les nouvelles juridictions constitutionnelles de Yougoslavie*, 15 (Nos. 1-3) LE NOUVEAU DROIT YOUGOSLAVE 21 ff. (1964). *See also* W. GELLHORN, OMBUDSMEN AND OTHERS 273-78 (Cambridge, Mass., Harvard University Press, 1966); Rozmaryn, *La Constitution, loi fondamentale de l'Etat socialiste*, in P. BISCARETTI DI RUFFÌA & S. ROZMARYN, LA CONSTITUTION COMME LOI FONDAMENTALE DANS LES ETATS DE L'EUROPE OCCIDENTALE ET DANS LES ETATS SOCIALISTES 111 f. (Torino & Paris, Giappichelli & Librarie Générale de Droit et de Jurisprudence, 1966); Franchi, *Note sulla giurisdizione costituzionale jugoslava*, 21 RIVISTA DI DIRITTO PROCESSUALE 397 ff. (1966); Lacy, *Yugoslavia: Practice and Procedure in a Communist Country*, 43 ORE. L. REV. 1, 13 f. (1963); Vigoriti, *La giurisdizione costituzionale in Jugoslavia*, 20 RIVISTA TRIMESTRALE DI DIRITTO E PROCEDURA CIVILE 298 ff. (1966). It is still too early to have a precise idea of the practical importance of this innovation in Yugoslavia. Judgment must be confined to the legislative texts (which in truth are rather complicated and sometimes ambiguous); in particular, to arts. 241-251 of the Federal Constitution of April 7, 1963 and to the "law on the Yugoslav Constitutional Court" of December 1963 (both are translated in INSTITUT DE DROIT COMPARÉ, 7 & 14 RECUEILS DES LOIS DE LA RSF DE YOUGOSLAVIE (Beograd, 1963 and 1965)). In some respects the Yugoslav institution would seem to be even more innovative than that adopted elsewhere in Europe; for example, art. 68, para. 3, of the law quoted above proclaims the right of minority judges to record their dissenting opinions. It remains unclear, however, whether a dissenting opinion can then be openly published or whether it is to be considered as a purely internal document of the court.

[21] *See* 2 THE FEDERALIST No. 78, at 294 (New York, 1788), cited and commented upon by C.L. BLACK, THE PEOPLE AND THE COURT. JUDICIAL REVIEW IN A DEMOCRACY 158, 229 (New York, Macmillan, 1960); Kadish, *supra* note 7, at 7 f.; Ch. II, note 5 *supra* and accompanying text.

case they are replaced by the obvious criterion of "lex superior derogat legi inferiori:" a constitutional norm, if the constitution is rigid, prevails over an ordinary legislative norm in conflict with it, just as ordinary legislation prevails over subordinate legislation,[22] or, as the Germans would say, *Gesetze* prevail over *Verordnungen*.[23]

e) Hence, one must conclude that *any* judge, having to decide a case where an applicable ordinary legislative norm conflicts with the Constitution, must disregard the former and apply the latter.[24]

§ 4. The rationale of centralized judicial review

This reasoning is so coherent and simple that one might well ask for what strange reason the Austrian Constitution of 1920-1929 preferred to establish a centralized system of judicial review;[25] and why this system has been adopted by the constitutions of several countries (all of the civil law tradition), including Czechoslovakia, Spain, Italy, Germany, Cyprus, Turkey and Yugoslavia.

But, despite possible logical inconsistencies, the solution adopted by the Austrian and then by the other constitutions mentioned above was not without its reasons. The following seem to be the most important.

---

[22] In Italy, for instance, administrative "regulations" have to be disregarded by the courts if contrary to the "laws." *See* art. 5 of the law of March 20, 1865, No. 2248, all. E; CALAMANDREI, *supra* note 2, at 8 f. (3 OPERE GIURIDICHE at 352). In France also, the *acte réglementaire illégal* has to be disregarded by the courts in consequence of an *exception d'illégalité*. The ordinary courts do not, however, annul such administrative acts with general effect, but can only disregard them for the case at hand. Nonetheless, this does not prevent an action before the *Conseil d'Etat* for annulment with general effect. *See* C.-A. COLLIARD, LIBERTÉS PUBLIQUES 142 f. (Paris, Dalloz, 3d ed. 1968).

[23] *See* Friesenhahn, *supra* note 12, at 144 f.

[24] A. DE TOCQUEVILLE, 1 DE LA DÉMOCRATIE EN AMÉRIQUE, Ch. VI, at 174 ff. (Bruxelles, Meline, Cans et Co., 1840), had already observed that, if the Constitution is "la première des lois" and cannot be changed by an ordinary law, the logical result is that the courts ought to obey the Constitution in preference to all other laws: "ceci tient à l'essence même du pouvoir judiciaire. Choisir entre les dispositions légales celles qui l'enchaînent le plus étroitement est, en quelque sorte, le droit naturel du magistrat" (at 179). The different French approach can be explained—according to the famous writer— on the basis of the "raison d'Etat" rather than the "raison ordinaire" (at 180) which has prevailed in the United States. The result is that in France, unlike the United States, the superiority of the Constitution is more nominal than effective: "en refusant aux juges le droit de déclarer les lois inconstitutionnelles, nous donnons indirectement au corps législatif le pouvoir de changer la constitution, puisqu'il ne rencontre plus de barrière légale qui l'arrête" (at 179).

[25] See on this point Melichar, *Die Verfassungsgerichtsbarkeit in Österreich*, in MAX-PLANCK-INSTITUT, *supra* note 7, at 445, 486 and *passim*.

a) The centralized system reflects a different conception of the separation of powers, and is based on a radically different doctrine from that upon which decentralized review is founded.

Under a centralized system one can no longer uphold the classic reasoning of Hamilton and Marshall, which tried to resolve the problem of unconstitutional laws and of judicial review purely in terms of statutory interpretation.

The civil law countries tend to adhere more rigidly to the doctrines of the separation of powers and the supremacy of statutory law. Originally these doctrines meant, to Montesquieu,[26] Rousseau, and others haunted by fears of a self-seeking, anti-democratic judiciary, that any judicial interpretation or, a fortiori, invalidation of statutes was a *political* act, and therefore an encroachment on the exclusive power of the legislative branch to make law.[27] Even today, although the advisability of some sort of control over the constitutionality of legislation is admitted, the essentially political aspects of this function are recognized.[28] Thus the centralized systems refuse to grant the judiciary in general the power to review legislation; in fact, the ordinary judges must accept and apply the law as they find it.[29] Several scholars have even, not without some justification, spoken of a genuine presumption of legislative validity.[30] The only attenuation of these notions lies in the power of the ordinary judges to suspend concrete litigation pending a reference to the Constitutional Court of a constitutional issue which has been raised. In Austria even this power is severely curtailed.[31]

---

[26] Diverging interpretations of Montesquieu's doctrine, formulated in L'Esprit des lois (1748), are well known. For a recent analysis see M.J.C. Vile, Constitutionalism and Separation of Powers 76-97, esp. 83, 86 ff. (Oxford, Clarendon Press, 1967). *See also* Eckhoff, *Impartiality, Separation of Powers, and Judicial Independence*, 9 Scandinavian Studies in Law 22 (1965).

[27] See generally Ch. II, §§ 4 and 5 *supra*, for the historical background of the distinction between the American version of separation of powers, which emphasizes preventing any excessive concentration of power in any one branch, through a system of *checks and balances*, and the traditional French concept which emphasizes a strict *separation* of functions and personnel. The presidential veto over legislation is an example of the American concept, while the historic attempts to prevent the French judiciary from even interpreting legislation are examples of the opposite philosophy. See also Ch. I, § 5 *supra*.

[28] *See* notes 64 and 65 *infra*, and accompanying text.

[29] *See*, for example, Melichar, *supra* note 25, at 445, 459 f.; Friesenhahn, *supra* note 12, at 136 f.

[30] *See*, for example, Cereti, *Funzione legislativa e controllo di legittimità*, 8 Rivista trimestrale di diritto pubblico 57 (1958). References and criticisms of the "presumption of the validity of legislation," a notion usually attributed to Laband, can be found in M. Cappelletti, La pregiudizialità costituzionale nel processo civile 84 ff. (Milano, Giuffrè, 1957); C. Esposito, La validità delle leggi 34 ff. (Milano, Giuffrè, 2d ed. 1964); Dietze, *supra* note 12, at 554.

[31] This subject will be further treated in Ch. IV *infra*.

This recognition of the political character of judicial review is reflected both in the manner of appointing the members of the special constitutional courts and in the sort of questions entertained by such courts. The agencies appointing the judges are usually prescribed by the constitution itself and an effort is made to ensure that the courts' membership reflects all major political groupings, so that the courts are "not the prolonged arm of some other state organ or of the political parties."[32] Similarly, the centralized constitutional courts do not shy away from considering issues which the Supreme Court of the United States would reject as essentially "political." The American Court has often avoided questions which it has called "political," for instance, issues regarding the executive's conduct of foreign relations, or concerning the legislature's observance of proper procedures in passing a statute or constitutional amendment.[33] In contrast, the continental courts, consistent with their admitted quasi-political function, may at times entertain such dangerous questions.[34] Nonetheless, such functions remain barred to the judiciary as a whole in these systems; in this way, they attempt to remain true to strict concepts of separation of powers.

b) The centralized system reflects the absence of the principle of stare decisis in civil law jurisdictions.

In the decentralized or American type of control all the judicial organs, federal and state, superior and inferior, have the power and duty to disregard unconstitutional legislation in the concrete

---

[32] Geck, *supra* note 7, at 258.

[33] This policy, grounded both in the conviction that some questions are better answered by other branches of the government and in a realistic desire to avoid provoking a direct clash with the other branches of government which could, after all, simply refuse to obey the courts, is facilitated by several doctrines: those of "ripeness," "case or controversy," "standing," "political question," etc. *See generally* SHAPIRO, *supra* note 4, at 174 ff.; Ch. IV, § 6 *infra*.

[34] Thus the European constitutional courts and the French *Conseil Constitutionnel* may be specifically charged with determining the constitutionality of political parties (art. 21, para. 2, of the German Basic Law of 1949) and the validity of elections (art. 41 of the German Basic Law and arts. 58-60 of the French Constitution of 1958), with deciding the most delicate conflicts of jurisdiction between legislature and executive (arts. 34, 37 and 61 of the 1958 French Constitution; art. 134 of the 1948 Italian Constitution; art. 93, paras. 1 and 3 of the German Basic Law), with deciding the validity of treaties (*see* Geck, *supra* note 7, at 265), etc. Also to be considered is the fact that the continental constitutional courts do not confine their deliberations to the facts of the specific case but rather tend to treat issues in the abstract, since they are obliged to make a final decision, regarding a given law, which will be valid *erga omnes*. Finally, the civil law jurisdictions do not have the certiorari device which permits the Supreme Court to refuse to hear cases which it may feel are too delicate to be decided at a given time. See *infra*, in this section, *sub c*.

cases which come before them. Yet the American system makes no explicit provision for decisions with *erga omnes* effects or formal declarations of invalidity of unconstitutional statutes. Since even in American courts, state and federal, there may be differences of opinion as to the constitutionality of a law, it might be asked how the citizenry can ever be sure what attitude a particular court will take toward a particular law. The answer is that the serious consequences of conflicts and uncertainty have been avoided in the United States, and in the other common law countries where the decentralized system of judicial review operates, through the basic principle of stare decisis, by force of which a decision by the highest court in any jurisdiction is binding on all lower courts in the same jurisdiction.[35] The exceptions to this general rule do not substantially affect the validity of our present argument, since the final result of the principle of binding precedents is that through the system of appeals the question of constitutionality can eventually be decided by the superior judicial organs and, in particular, by the Supreme Court, whose decision will be binding on all other courts. Thus the principle of stare decisis means that a judgment of unconstitutionality will become effective, practically speaking, *erga omnes*.

A decision is not limited to the case at hand; hence it bars a contrary decision in other cases.[36] An American law which has not

---

[35] *See* BROSSARD, *supra* note 7, at 153; M.A. FRANKLIN, THE DYNAMICS OF AMERICAN LAW 211 f., 295-319, 388, 569 f. (Mineola, N.Y., Foundation Press, 1968); Cappelletti & Adams, *supra* note 10, at 1215. In Mexico there have been attempts to arrive at similar results and to avoid the difficulties mentioned in the text. Thus there has been a limited binding force given to precedents (the "jurisprudencia") of the *Suprema Corte de Justicia de la Nación* (*see* M. Cappelletti, under *Amparo*, in 2 ENCICLOPEDIA DEL DIRITTO 330 (Milano, Giuffrè, 1958)). Also there has been the new institution of the "suplencia de la queja deficiente," which, I am told, has been scarcely used; notwithstanding the individual effects of judgments of unconstitutionality, a Mexican court may draw the plaintiff's attention to the fact that the state action, which is the subject of the plaintiff's claim, has already been declared unconstitutional in prior decisions of the *Suprema Corte*. See J.V. CASTRO, LA SUPLENCIA DE LA QUEJA DEFICIENTE EN EL JUICIO DE AMPARO, esp. 59 f. (México, Editorial Jus, 1953); FIX ZAMUDIO, *supra* note 3, at 190, 403 f., 406-08; Ch. V, text and note 5 *infra*.

[36] The rule of stare decisis is not only generally less strictly observed in America than in England, but in America it is less strictly adhered to in constitutional cases than in others. This is the result of the more dynamic nature and greater flexibility of constitutional law which demands more creative interpretation. *See* Justice Brandeis' dissent in Burnet v. Colorado Oil and Gas Co., 285 U.S. 393, 406-08 (1932); and FRANKLIN, *supra* note 35, at 211 f., 295-319, 388, 569 f.; Kadish, *supra* note 7, 152 esp. n.82. Yet, it is interesting to note that the fundamentally important result of changing what would be a mere *cognitio incidentalis* of unconstitutionality, valid only for the particular case, into a statement of the law with validity *erga omnes*, has been achieved through the rule of stare decisis. It would, therefore, seem to me to be difficult

been applied because found to be unconstitutional by the Supreme Court remains "on the books." Yet it becomes "dead law,"[37] though there may have been certain rare cases of the revival of such a law after a change of course by the Supreme Court.[38]

In this way the simple reasoning of Hamilton in the *Federalist* and of Marshall in *Marbury v. Madison* has had more far-reaching effects than would at first have been imagined. In truth, this reasoning tended to resolve the problem of unconstitutionality of legislation in terms of pure and simple statutory interpretation. Since, the argument ran, the Constitution is a "stronger" law, the judge, having to decide a case where the applicable law is in his opinion unconstitutional, must give precedence to the Constitution. The judge does not invade the realm of the legislative power; he is not attempting to legislate. He simply disregards the "lower" law in the concrete case.[39] However, through the instrument of stare decisis,

---

to agree with certain attempts, both old and recent, to deny or modify excessively the importance of stare decisis as one of the elements differentiating the so-called Anglo-Saxon systems from the continental ones (see, for example, Ancel, *Réflexions sur l'étude comparative des Cours suprêmes et le "Recours en Cassation,"* in 1 ANNALES DE L'INSTITUT DE DROIT COMPARÉ DE L'UNIVERSITÉ DE PARIS 301 (1934); Zajtav, *Begriff, System und Präjudiz in den kontinentalen Rechten und im Common Law,* 165 ARCHIV FÜR DIE CIVILISTISCHE PRAXIS 103 ff. (1965)). When one asserts, as many have done (see, for example, WOLF, *supra* note 9, at 215), that "in the field of constitutional law the principle of stare decisis has been practically suppressed," this is only half the truth. It is true that the Supreme Court has been assuming the right to change its own legal doctrines and hence to go against previous decisions. But, on the other hand, there can be no doubt that the decisions of the Supreme Court itself are considered as fully binding and are followed by the lower courts and other public organs.

[37] Kauper, *Judicial Review of Constitutional Issues in the United States,* in MAX-PLANCK-INSTITUT, *supra* note 7, at 611, 629; Cappelletti & Adams, *supra* note 10, at 1215; see references in Prakke, *Reflections on Judicial Review of Legislation,* 4 ACTA POLITICA. TIJDSCHRIFT VOOR POLITICOLOGIE 418 f. (1969). The same is true for Canada; *cf.* BROSSARD, *supra* note 7, at 151-55, 235 f.

[38] Much more frequent has been the reverse: judgments holding unconstitutional a law previously held to be constitutional.

One scholar sees no reason in principle why a statute cannot be revived after being declared unconstitutional. Nimmer, *A Proposal for Judicial Validation of a Previously Unconstitutional Law: The Civil Rights Act of 1875,* 65 COLUM. L. REV. 1394 (1965). However, perhaps the only instance of such a revival is *In re* Rahrer, 140 U.S. 545 (1891). The Supreme Court upheld a Kansas statute it had formerly declared unconstitutional as an infringement of congressional power under the commerce clause. In the time between the two decisions, Congress authorized such state action. The Court said that the Kansas statute became effective immediately after this authorization, without the Kansas legislature reenacting the statute. Also of interest is the opinion of the Attorney General that the District of Columbia minimum wage law, ruled unconstitutional in Adkins v. Children's Hospital, 261 U.S. 525 (1923), automatically came back into force when the Supreme Court reversed this case in West Coast Hotel Co. v. Parrish, 300 U.S. 379 (1937). 39 Opinions Atty. Gen. 22 (1937).

[39] *See* ESPOSITO, *supra* note 30, at 21 ff.; Kadish, *supra* note 7, at 8 (quoting Hamilton); § 3 *supra*.

this "non-application" in the particular case becomes in practice a genuine quashing of the unconstitutional law which is final, definite and valid for every future case. In short, it becomes a true annulment of the law with, at least in theory, retroactive effects.[40]

Since the principle of stare decisis is foreign to civil law judges,[41] a system which allowed each judge to decide on the constitutionality of statutes could result in a law being disregarded as unconstitutional by some judges, while being held constitutional and applied by others. Furthermore, the same judicial organ, which had one day disregarded a given law, might uphold it the next day, having changed its mind about the law's constitutional legitimacy.[42] Differences could arise between judicial bodies of different type or degree, for example between ordinary courts and administrative tribunals,[43] or between the younger, more radical judges of the inferior courts and the older, more tradition conscious judges of the higher courts. This is notoriously what happened in Italy from 1948 to 1956 and what continues to happen on a large scale in Japan.[44] The extremely dangerous result could be a serious conflict between the judicial organs and grave uncertainty as to the law. Moreover, even though a given law has been held unconstitutional with regard to one party, nevertheless other affected parties would

---

[40] On this subject see Ch. V *infra*.

[41] One can well say that the rule of stare decisis is foreign to the spirit of civil law systems, while recognizing the prime importance of judicial decisions as informal sources of law (the so-called *auctoritas rerum similiter judicatarum*). It is true that in a few civil law countries a binding force was or still is given to precedents, but this practice has been always by way of exception and without any notable degree of practical success. Thus the French *Parlements* before the Revolution not only introduced a type of judicial review (see Ch. II, § 4 *supra*), but may also have formulated a doctrine of the binding force of precedents; the doctrine, however, was suppressed by the Revolution. *See* R. DAVID & H.P. DE VRIES, THE FRENCH LEGAL SYSTEM 113 (New York, Oceana, 1958). For other more recent (Hungary) or still valid (Spain) examples of civil law systems in which judicial decisions are or were binding, at least in part, see Zajtay, *supra* note 36, at 97, 103 and notes 30, 31; R. DAVID, LES GRANDS SYSTÈMES DE DROIT CONTEMPORAINS (DROIT COMPARÉ) 141 and references (Paris, Dalloz, 3d ed. 1969).

[42] *See* F. Pierandrei, under *Corte costituzionale*, in 10 ENCICLOPEDIA DEL DIRITTO esp. 881, 886 f. (Milano, Giuffrè, 1962); Biscaretti di Ruffia, *La Constitution, en tant que loi fondamentale, en Europe occidentale*, in BISCARETTI DI RUFFÌA & ROZMARYN, *supra* note 20, at 72 f.; Azzariti, *supra* note 5, at 9; Engelhardt, *supra* note 2, at 108.

[43] Engelhardt, *supra* note 2, at 108, rightly points out (also on the basis of the Greek experience, to which we might add the Italian one of 1948-1956) that in countries where, unlike the United States, separate courts deal with administrative law, a great danger arises which the American system avoids. This is the danger of conflicts between the ordinary courts and the administrative courts, culminating in conflicts between the two respective supreme organs.

[44] *See* Kiyomiya, *supra* note 8, at 336 f.; Abe, *supra* note 8, at 537.

have to raise the issue of constitutionality *de novo*. A Japanese writer offers a typical example, Japan being precisely one of the countries where, it appears, the gravity of these disadvantages is becoming increasingly evident.[45] A plaintiff files suit claiming that a certain tax law is unconstitutional and obtains a judgment to that effect; but, the writer continues, "according to the individual-effect theory, the law per se remains in force and binding on taxation offices." As a result, every other interested party must initiate a separate action to escape the effects of the law.[46]

And so, though the "American" system has been introduced in several civil law countries, it has not been an unqualified success.[47] Weimar Germany, and post-war Italy prior to the institution of its Constitutional Court, fully revealed the unsuitability of the decentralized method for civil law countries; and the same may be said for Japan. In Norway, Denmark, and Sweden, on the other hand, the problem is not acute, but only because decentralized judicial review is relatively unimportant and the judges exercise the power with extreme prudence and moderation.[48] In other civil law countries, this type of judicial review has not been successful, with the possible exception of Switzerland where the type of judicial review adopted is much more of a compromise between the two systems.[49]

---

[45] *See* Hayashida, *supra* note 8, at 424 f.

[46] One might take issue with the theory that a law remains binding on the public administration, although considered unconstitutional by the public administration itself. Hayashida states that "regarding the executive, even if the cabinet considers a law unconstitutional, it shall hold itself responsible to the Diet for any failure to apply and administer the law as long as it remains in force." (*Id.* at 425.) However, such a discussion would have little practical value. In fact, this theory, which I believe is unfounded, is commonly accepted not only in Japan but also in Italy and other countries despite the "rigid" nature of the Constitution. See the criticisms in CAPPELLETTI, *supra* note 30, at 76 ff., 84 ff.

[47] *See* Cappelletti & Adams, *supra* note 10, at 1213 ff.

[48] On the minor practical importance of judicial review in the Scandinavian countries see CASTBERG, DIE ZUSTÄNDIGKEIT, *supra* note 10, at 10; J.A. STORING, NORWEGIAN DEMOCRACY 156 (London, Allen & Unwin, 1963); Castberg, *Verfassungsgerichtsbarkeit, supra* note 10, at 417, 420; Eckhoff, *supra* note 26, at 28. *See also* DANISH AND NORWEGIAN LAW. A GENERAL SURVEY 13 (edited by the Danish Committee on Comparative Law, Copenhagen, Gad, 1963); Engelhardt, *supra* note 2, at 104.

[49] As for Switzerland, it would not be right to speak of a failure of the system adopted there. But one might add that it would be possible to agree with one Swiss writer who holds that in Switzerland, unlike in the United States, judicial review has never become "ein führendes verfassungsrechtliches Prinzip." GROSSMANN, *supra* note 9, at VIII. In fact the success of the Swiss system is due much less to the "decentralized" power of control outlined above and much more to the remedy of *staatsrechtliche Beschwerde* upon which only the Federal Tribunal is competent to judge (*see* note 9 and accompanying text *supra*). Thus, in this more important aspect, Swiss law actually presents us with a system of centralized rather than decentralized control.

Accordingly, in establishing a system of judicial review, the countries to whom the notion of stare decisis was foreign had to work with legal instruments very different from those of the United States and other common law countries. In the former countries it was thought essential to find an adequate substitute for the American Supreme Court. The need was felt for a judicial body capable of giving decisions of general binding effect in cases dealing with the constitutionality of legislation. It was hoped that such special bodies could avoid the conflicts and chaotic uncertainties of which we have spoken above.

Faced with this need, the "Fathers" of the Austrian Constitution decided to establish the *Verfassungsgerichtshof*, a special Constitutional Court.[50] The same solution was chosen at the same time in Czechoslovakia[51] and subsequently in Spain,[52] Italy,[53] Germany,[54] and in the three previously mentioned states which have only recently adopted centralized judicial review[55] where the controlling power is confined to one judicial organ specifically created for this function.

c) The centralized system reflects the unsuitability of traditional civil law courts for judicial review.

The American Supreme Court, and, for example, its Japanese counterpart under the Constitution of 1947[56] are far from being the equivalents of the European constitutional courts. While the latter concern themselves solely with constitutional questions, the jurisdiction of the Supreme Court in the United States is not so

---

See *id.* at 3 f.; GIACOMETTI, *supra* note 9, at 6 f., 14. Note also that judgments of unconstitutionality emanating from the Swiss Federal Tribunal have general binding effect. See G.A. CODDING JR., THE FEDERAL GOVERNMENT OF SWITZERLAND 102 f., 106 (Boston, Houghton Mifflin, 1961); F. FLEINER & Z. GIACOMETTI, SCHWEIZERISCHES BUNDESSTAATSRECHT 887 f., 897 f. (Zürich, Polygraphischer Verlag, 1949); W.J. WAGNER, THE FEDERAL STATES AND THEIR JUDICIARY (A COMPARATIVE STUDY IN CONSTITUTIONAL LAW AND ORGANISATION OF COURTS IN FEDERAL STATES) 109 (The Hague, Mouton, 1959); CAPPELLETTI, *supra* note 9, at 35; Imboden, *supra* note 9, at 516.

[50] Arts. 137-148 of the Austrian *Bundesverfassungsgesetz*.

[51] Art. 102 of the Czech Constitution of 1920. See Deener, *supra* note 13, at 1086.

[52] See note 15 and accompanying text *supra*.

[53] Arts. 134-137 of the Constitution of the Italian Republic.

[54] Arts. 92-94, 98-100, 126 of the Bonn Constitution.

[55] See notes 18, 19, 20 and accompanying text *supra*. There are in fact some anomalies in the systems adopted in these countries; one is revealed by comparing art. 144, para. 3, with art. 148 of the Constitution of the Republic of Cyprus. See Blümel, *supra* note 18, at 681 ff. See *also* Bernhardt, *Vergleichende Sachberichte: Normenkontrolle,* in MAX-PLANCK-INSTITUT, *supra* note 7, at 736 f., text and nn.109-110.

[56] *Cf.* J.M. MAKI, COURT AND CONSTITUTION IN JAPAN. SELECTED SUPREME COURT DECISIONS 1948-1960, at XV and *passim* (Seattle, University of Washington Press, 1964); Hayashida, *supra* note 8, at 421 ff.

confined, since most cases arise through the normal appellate system and not through any ad hoc procedure.[57] Even for constitutional questions no special procedure is used; to view such writs as habeas corpus, certiorari, or the writ of error as the basis of judicial review is a fundamental, though rather frequent, error.[58] Thus the Supreme Court should be compared not to the special constitutional courts, but rather to the highest courts of appeal on the continent, such as the Austrian *Oberster Gerichtshof,* the German *Bundesgerichtshof,* or the Italian *Corte di cassazione.*

At this point one might inquire why those countries which decided to have a centralized system of judicial review wanted to create special constitutional courts, and did not grant jurisdiction over constitutional matters to the already existing highest courts of appeal.[59] Constitutional jurisdiction might have been granted to these courts alone, without authorizing all judges to review legislation. Furthermore, one of the inherent difficulties of judicial review in a civil law country might have been overcome by making decisions of constitutionality issued by these courts binding on all inferior courts. The Swiss Federal Tribunal could have provided a useful precedent for such a scheme.[60]

---

[57] For development of this point see Ch. IV *infra.*

[58] GRANT, *supra* note 1, at 34.

Formally, the American Supreme Court is a court of ordinary jurisdiction. However, it is important to note that in practice it has increasingly assumed a position not very dissimilar from that occupied by the European constitutional courts. In fact, there is a tendency to limit the Supreme Court's activities to important constitutional matters and to the resolution of federal-state conflicts. On this development see note 81 *infra;* P.A. FREUND, THE SUPREME COURT OF THE UNITED STATES. ITS BUSINESS, PURPOSES AND PERFORMANCE 183 (Cleveland–New York, The World Publishing Co., 1961); Taft, *The Jurisdiction of the Supreme Court Under the Act of February 13, 1925,* 35 YALE L.J. 2 f. (1925); McWhinney, *Federal Constitutional Courts and Their Judges, as Instruments of a Democratic Polity,* in DIE MODERNE DEMOKRATIE UND IHR RECHT, *supra* note 8, at 516. "We have seen that, broadly speaking, the Supreme Court is now confined in its adjudications to questions of constitutionality and like problems of essentially national importance. . . . It was not always thus." Frankfurter & Landis, *The Business of the Supreme Court of the United States—A Study in the Federal Judicial System, Part VIII,* 40 HARV. L. REV. 1110, 1111 (1927).

[59] Moreover, one might ask why the centralized system on the European model has been suggested even for Japan by some of the several critics of the "American" method adopted in that country since 1947. *See* Kiyomiya, *supra* note 8, at 336; Hayashida, *supra* note 8, at 426 and note. *See also* note 8 *supra.*

[60] *See* notes 9 and 49 *supra.* The system introduced by art. 34 of the Irish Constitution of July 1, 1937, could also have been an interesting precedent: note 5 *supra.* The same might be said of certain countries in Latin America, such as Uruguay, where control of constitutionality is concentrated exclusively in the ordinary Supreme Court, the lower judges being bound to suspend the particular case in which the constitutional question arises. However, the judgments of the Supreme Court of Uruguay are not valid *erga*

But despite their theoretical suitability, the traditional highest courts of most civil law countries were found to lack the structure, procedures, and mentality required for an effective control over the constitutionality of legislation.

The European "supreme courts" lack the compact, manageable structure of the United States Supreme Court. Typical is Germany where there are no less than five high courts, one each for ordinary civil and criminal questions, administrative matters, tax disputes, labor problems, and controversies involving social legislation.[61] Even within a given high court there are several different divisions *(Senate)*, each with many members who sit and decide cases independently of the other divisions. It is difficult to imagine how, amidst such a welter of judges and jurisdictions, a consistent and carefully considered constitutional jurisprudence could ever be devised.[62]

Procedurally these courts of last instance are also handicapped by their frequent lack of any discretionary power to refuse jurisdiction, of a device similar to the certiorari of the United States Supreme Court. To illustrate, the Italian Court of Cassation must hear every case brought before it, an average of three to four thousand civil cases per year, while the Italian Constitutional Court delivers fewer than two hundred judgments annually. Thus, if the Court of Cassation were to have jurisdiction over constitutional cases as well, such cases would represent a fairly insignificant portion of its workload. Thus submerged, these cases would receive neither the time nor the consideration that they require. The situation is very similar for the superior courts of other civil law countries, such as Germany.

Lastly, the bulk of Europe's judiciary seems psychologically incapable of the value-oriented, quasi-political functions involved in

---

omnes but are confined to the concrete case, so that the effectiveness of the system—given the lack of stare decisis—is severely limited. *Cf.* VESCOVI, *supra* note 1, at 36 f., 47 f., 61 ff. and *passim*. For the Canadian system see note 7 *supra*.

[61] *See* E.J. COHN, MANUAL OF GERMAN LAW 36 (Dobbs Ferry, N.Y., Oceana, 1968); F. Baur, *Introduction* to BIBLIOGRAPHY OF GERMAN LAW: BIBLIOGRAPHIE DES DEUTSCHEN RECHTS 34 ff. (Karlsruhe, C.F. Müller, 1964). In general on the highest courts in various countries, see J. MAGNUS, DIE HÖCHSTEN GERICHTE DER WELT (Leipzig, Moeser, 1929).

[62] Furthermore, since more judges belong to a division than are required to decide a single case, the individual judges called to take part in decisions by the division may vary from case to case. Consider, for example, that a few hundred judges belong to the Italian Court of Cassation. *See* G. DI FEDERICO, LA GIUSTIZIA COME ORGANIZZAZIONE: LA CORTE DI CASSAZIONE 55 ff. (Bari, Laterza, 1969).

judicial review.[63] It should be borne in mind that continental judges usually are "career judges," who enter the judiciary at a very early age and are promoted to the higher courts largely on the basis of seniority. Their professional training develops skills in technical rather than policy-oriented application of statutes. The exercise of judicial review, however, is rather different from the usual judicial function of applying the law.[64] Modern constitutions do not limit themselves to a fixed definition of what the law is, but contain broad programs for future action. Therefore the task of fulfilling the constitution often demands a higher sense of discretion than the task of interpreting ordinary statutes; that is certainly one reason why Kelsen, Calamandrei, and others have considered it to be a legislative rather than a purely judicial activity.[65]

In the United States, the Supreme Court itself first undertook the task of judicial review, but to impose this function on European superior courts, to whom such an activity would be unfamiliar and foreign to their traditions, was not considered suitable. In fact, these considerations had been amply borne out in practice. We have already noted that both Weimar Germany,[66] and Italy from 1948 to 1956,[67] experimented with the decentralized system of judicial review. Since the power was exercised by all the courts, cases came in the last instance before the *Reichsgericht* or the *Corte di cassazione*, the highest ordinary courts in the respective

---

[63] This seems equally true for Yugoslavia, the first Communist country to adopt judicial review. GELLHORN, *supra* note 20, at 273 n.43, indicates that Marshall Tito's government was readily won over to the idea of judicial review. However, the lawyers and judges of the Supreme Court opposed it, and were almost impossible to win over.

[64] This subject has been much discussed. *See, e.g.,* Cappelletti, *L'attività e i poteri del giudice costituzionale in rapporto con il loro fine generico,* in 3 SCRITTI GIURIDICI IN MEMORIA DI P. CALAMANDREI 83-164 (Padova, Cedam, 1958); Leibholz, *Das Spannungsverhältnis von Politik und Recht und die Integrationsfunktion des Bundesverfassungsgerichtes,* in INTEGRITAS—GEISTIGE WANDLUNG UND MENSCHLICHE WIRKLICHKEIT 211 ff. (D. Stolte & R. Wisser (eds.), Tübingen, Rainer Wunderlich Verlag, n.d.); Zweigert, *Zum richterlichen Charisma in einer ethisierten Rechtsordnung,* in FESTGABE FÜR CARLO SCHMID 299, 303-05 (Tübingen, Mohr, 1962); Kirchheimer, *Prinzipien der Verfassungsinterpretation in den Vereinigten Staaten,* 11 JAHRBUCH DES ÖFFENTLICHEN RECHTS DER GEGENWART 93 ff., esp. 97 ff. (1962). *See generally* F.V. CAHILL, JR., JUDICIAL LEGISLATION, esp. 46 ff. (New York, Ronald Press, 1952); G. ROELLECKE, POLITIK UND VERFASSUNGSGERICHTSBARKEIT (Heidelberg, Verlagsgesellschaft "Recht und Wirtschaft," 1961); Bachof, *Der Verfassungsrichter zwischen Recht und Politik,* in SUMMUM IUS SUMMA INIURIA 41 ff. (Tübingen, Mohr, 1963).

[65] See also for the references, Cappelletti, *Il controllo di costituzionalità delle leggi nel quadro delle funzioni dello Stato,* 15 RIVISTA DI DIRITTO PROCESSUALE 376 ff., esp. 384 ff. (1960).

[66] § 2, text and note 12 *supra.*

[67] § 2, text and note 13 *supra.*

countries. In Germany, however, the system certainly did not produce satisfactory results.[68] In Italy, the Court of Cassation, often with the acquiescence of the *Consiglio di Stato,* used its powers of interpretation much more in the sense of "unfulfilling" the Constitution than of fulfilling it.[69] During these eight years, the Court of Cassation, even more than other courts, gave the best possible proof of its unsuitability to judge constitutional questions. Apparently the long traditions of this Court, with the professional deformation of its elderly career judges, instead of being of benefit were much more of a handicap to the Court in its new role.[70]

Nor are such practical confirmations of the unsuitability of decentralized review in civil law countries confined to Germany and Italy. In the Scandinavian countries, the modest role of the Supreme Court, and of the judiciary in general, in matters of judicial review is generally recognized.[71] In Japan it appears that in the first twenty years after the promulgation of the Constitution, the Japanese Supreme Court has found statutes unconstitutional in, at best, two cases; and in only one of these situations was the statute in question still in effect at the time of the decision.[72] This may be attributable to the way of thinking of the career judges in that Court.

---

[68] *See* CATINELLA, *supra* note 13, at 118 ff.; H. SCHORN, DER RICHTER IM DRITTEN REICH 23 (Frankfurt a.M., Klostermann, 1959); SPANNER, *supra* note 12, at 4-6, 22-28, 38; Dietze, *supra* note 12, at 545-47.

[69] See the forceful description in Calamandrei, *Come si fa a disfare una Costituzione,* in DIECI ANNI DOPO: 1945-1955, at 209-316 (Bari, Laterza, 1955), republished in 3 OPERE GIURIDICHE, *supra* note 2, at 511 ff.

[70] It might not be too presumptuous to suppose that the French Court of Cassation would not have been much more sensitive to problems of legislative constitutionality than its Italian counterpart. In fact, on several occasions not only academic thought, *e.g.,* such well-known figures as Hauriou, Duguit, Jèze and Duverger (see Ch. I, text and notes 5 and 6 *supra*), but even some inferior tribunals have moved a bit towards affirming a decentralized judicial power to control legislation in France. But, as two French constitutional lawyers make clear, "la Cour de Cassation et le Conseil d'Etat se refusent inébranlablement à examiner le moyen d'inconstitutionnalité d'une disposition législative, que des plaideurs invoquent parfois à l'appui de leur cause." Eisenmann & Hamon, *La Juridiction Constitutionnelle en Droit Français (1875-1961),* in MAX-PLANCK-INSTITUT, *supra* note 7, at 240. G. Vedel also speaks of "une certaine insensibilité du Conseil d'Etat aux innovations constitutionnelles" in his *Préface* to FRANCINE BATAILLER, LE CONSEIL D'ETAT JUGE CONSTITUTIONNEL IV (Paris, Pichon et Durand-Auzias, 1966). One can find analogous circumstances in Belgium. P. WIGNY, 1 DROIT CONSTITUTIONNEL §§ 103-104 (Bruxelles, Bruylant, 1952); 2 *id.* § 604.

[71] § 4(b), text and note 48 *supra.*

[72] *Cf.* Kiyomiya, *supra* note 8, at 336; MAKI, *supra* note 56, at XXX, XLIII; Henderson, *supra* note 8, at 1016 ff. Bibliographical materials do not, however, fully clarify this point. One or two cases are mentioned in Ito, *The Rule of Law: Constitutional Development,* in LAW IN JAPAN: THE LEGAL ORDER IN A CHANGING SOCIETY 205, 238 text and note (A.T. von Mehren (ed.), Cambridge, Mass., Harvard University Press, 1963); Nathanson, *supra* note 8, at 202, 216. *See also* T. MCNELLY, CONTEMPORARY GOVERNMENT OF

Finally, in Switzerland the success of the *Tribunal fédéral* in matters of judicial review confirms, rather than denies, this observation, if one remembers that that court is composed of twenty-six judges who are not career judges but elected by the Federal Assembly.[73]

The Justices of the Supreme Court of the United States, on the other hand, would seem in the light of almost two centuries of experience to have demonstrated, on the whole, their suitability for their delicate task. While the Court has often reached results that many would condemn, it has not suffered from the hesitancy and unfamiliarity with constitutional adjudication of European decentralized systems. Indeed, some of the greatest names in American history have been those of Justices of the Supreme Court. This fact is, of course, due to various circumstances, but one that deserves emphasizing is that judicial review was a product of the Supreme Court itself. It may be said that the Court has necessarily had to achieve a high level of performance, in order to fulfill a function with which the courage of its early Justices had endowed it. Furthermore, there is the fact that the members of that Court—and the same applies to the other federal courts—are not "career" judges, as is the usual case with the ordinary European judges. They are politically appointed, not necessarily from the ranks of the lower courts.

These, then, seem to be the most important reasons why, when adopting judicial review, several civil law countries (Austria, Germany, Italy, etc.) chose not to use existing judicial organs and the

---

JAPAN 168 (London, Allen & Unwin, 1963), who explains that "the Supreme Court [of Japan], with the exception of certain laws passed to implement Occupation directives, has never held any law, order, regulation, or official act unconstitutional." Nor does the situation seem to have improved in recent years judging by what a Japanese colleague wrote in 1966: "bisher wurden nur ein Gesetz, eine Verordnung und zwei Urteile der unteren Gerichte durch den Obersten Gerichtshof als verfassungswidrig erklärt"; Abe, *supra* note 8, at 537. *See also* DAVID, *supra* note 41, at 552, where one reads that in Japan "le contrôle de la constitutionnalité est exercé avec beaucoup de prudence, sinon de réticence, par le tribunal suprême." A.T. von Mehren, in LAW IN JAPAN, *supra*, at 424, writes that the Supreme Court of Japan "is composed of fifteen justices, of whom five are . . . to be career judges and five lawyers. Both the conception of the law held by this group and its conditioning experiences lead the lawyers and career judges to be hesitant to declare legislation unconstitutional or to interfere with governmental process on constitutional grounds"; and at 422 he expresses the fear that the Japanese Supreme Court interprets "too broadly" the notion of "nonjusticiable political question" to the detriment of the fundamental rights of man. One should notice, however, that there may well be a future evolutionary tendency on the part of the Japanese Supreme Court. This tendency in fact seems already to be manifested in the frequent dissenting opinions of judges of that Court.

[73] Election is for a term of six years; however, they are usually re-elected. *See* CODDING, *supra* note 49, at 103; Zellweger, *The Swiss Federal Court as a Constitutional Court of Justice,* 7 (No. 1) JOURNAL OF THE INTERNATIONAL COMMISSION OF JURISTS 101 (1966). See also note 49 *supra*.

members of the professional judiciary. Rather, they preferred to
introduce entirely new and special judicial bodies, despite the
serious problems of coordination arising from this choice.[74] Naturally
these special courts, as all the other judicial organs, have full independence and autonomy. However, their members (or at least
the majority of them) are not career judges, but, following the
analogy of the American Supreme Court,[75] are selected from diverse
backgrounds and appointed by the highest legislative or executive
organs of the State.[76]

§ 5.   Converging trends

For the sake of clarity a dichotomy has been drawn between
"centralized" and "decentralized" forms of judicial review, a dichotomy which in fact exaggerates the differences between the two
systems. For the sake of balance, several points of convergence be-

---

[74] On the problems of coordinating the work of a constitutional court with
that of the other courts see especially Calamandrei, *Corte costituzionale e
Autorità giudiziaria*, 11 (part 1) RIVISTA DI DIRITTO PROCESSUALE 7 ff. (1956),
republished in 3 OPERE GIURIDICHE, *supra* note 2, at 609 ff.; Merryman &
Vigoriti, *When Courts Collide: Constitution and Cassation in Italy*, 15 AM. J.
COMP. L. 665 ff. (1967). In addition, the creation of a "sovereign" constitutional court cannot but raise further problems of coordination vis-à-vis the
other state powers and organs. *See, e.g.*, P. BARILE, *La Corte costituzionale or-
gano sovrano: implicazioni pratiche*, in SCRITTI DI DIRITTO COSTITUZIONALE 226 ff.
(Padova, Cedam, 1967); P. BARILE, *Legami fra la Corte costituzionale e le
funzioni esecutiva e legislativa e influenza di queste su quella*, in SCRITTI DI DI-
RITTO COSTITUZIONALE, *supra* at 444 ff.
[75] The same can be said of the Mexican *Suprema Corte de Justicia de la
Nación. See* arts. 94-96 of the Mexican Constitution.
[76] *See* the Austrian Constitution, art. 147; the Italian Constitution, art. 135;
the Bonn Constitution, art. 94. Briefly, the Austrian *Verfassungsgerichtshof* is
composed of 14 judges (plus 6 substitutes), 8 of these (plus 3 substitutes)
being nominated by the President of the Republic after proposals by the
Cabinet; the other 6 (plus 3 substitutes) are also nominated by the President of the Republic but selected from a list submitted by both Houses of
Parliament. The Italian *Corte costituzionale* is composed of 15 judges, one
third of whom are nominated by the President of the Republic, one third by
Parliament and one third by the higher civil, penal and administrative courts.
The German *Bundesverfassungsgericht* is composed of 16 judges nominated
by Parliament, half being chosen by the *Bundestag* and half by the *Bundesrat*.
In all three countries the choice must be made from lawyers, that is to say
from persons who, apart from other requirements such as age, etc., have
completed regular studies in law. For further details see FRIEDRICH, *supra*
note 12, at 86; Engelhardt, *supra* note 2, at 110 ff.; Geck, *supra* note 7, at
258-62.
    The Turkish system of nominating judges to the Constitutional Court is
very similar to the Italian one. *See* art. 145 of the Turkish Constitution of
1961 and *see, e.g.*, Azrak, *supra* note 19, at 79 f. In Yugoslavia the President
and the ten judges of the Constitutional Court are elected by the Federal
Assembly on the proposal of the President of the Republic (art. 217, para. 1,
No. 2, and art. 164, para. 1, No. 6 of the Yugoslav Constitution. See also
art. 243).

tween the two approaches should now be re-emphasized. The twentieth century has blurred long-standing distinctions between the natural law and the positive law,[77] between precedent-oriented and statute-oriented courts, and between varying separation of powers theories, distinctions which lay at the bottom of the assumed differences in attitude toward judicial review.

The very establishment of special constitutional courts with the power to review and invalidate statutes for failure to conform with the constitution was, of course, a considerable compromise with that conception of the separation of powers which would deny such a power to all judicial organs.[78] True, the ordinary courts remain barred from judicial review in countries with a centralized system of control. However, even in these countries the ordinary courts have a role to play in this task. They often must make the initial judgment as to whether a constitutional issue ought to be referred to the special court.[79] This duty, as well as the obligation to recognize the binding effects of constitutional court decisions,[80] may help to stimulate a "constitutional consciousness" in the European judiciary similar to that which has been found for nearly two centuries in its American counterpart.

Nor is the movement toward convergence confined to the European side of the Atlantic. Through the use of certiorari, the United States Supreme Court is gradually confining itself to only the most significant—mostly constitutionally grounded—questions;[81] this is, of course, the exact role of the European constitutional

---

[77] See Ch. II *supra.*

[78] See note 26 and accompanying text *supra;* Azzariti, *supra* note 5, at 40 f. The *judicial* nature of the special constitutional courts is explicitly recognized in art. 92 of the Bonn Constitution, which declares that "die rechtsprechende Gewalt ist den Richtern anvertraut; sie wird *durch das Bundesverfassungsgericht,* durch das Oberste Bundesgericht, durch die in diesem Grundgesetze vorgesehenen Bundesgerichte und durch die Gerichte der Länder ausgeübt." The same idea can be seen implicitly in art. 140, sec. VI, of the Austrian Constitution. *See* Ermacora, *Die österreichische Verfassungsgerichtsbarkeit seit 1945,* 8 JAHRBUCH DES ÖFFENTLICHEN RECHTS DER GEGENWART 54, 61 (1959) with other references; Geck, *supra* note 7, at 257. One might also note that the recent Turkish Constitution deals with the Constitutional Court in the section devoted to the judicial power; *see, e.g.,* Azrak, *supra* note 19, at 76 f., 80 f.

[79] See Ch. IV *infra.*

[80] See Ch. V *infra.*

[81] See note 58 *supra;* Ch. IV, note 42 and accompanying text *infra.* In 1950, 33% of the cases decided by the Supreme Court involved constitutional questions as a principal issue. In 1955, this percentage was 29%; in 1960, it was 35%; in 1965, it was 39%. In 1966, 1967 and 1968 constitutional questions were the principal issues in 47%, 46%, and 54% of the cases, respectively. (Statistics taken from the yearly compilations in *Harvard Law Review,* published each November.)

courts which have no jurisdiction at all in "ordinary" cases. Likewise, the role of the American Supreme Court is now openly admitted to be partly political. Its membership has always been specially appointed by a popularly elected president, and recent confirmation hearings by the Senate show an increasing recognition of the highly political functions of the high court. Nor does the court seem to avoid politically delicate questions as zealously as it once did, as is illustrated by the racial discrimination and reapportionment decisions.[82]

Judicial review in the world today is, therefore, a continuum ranging from those countries, like the Soviet Union, whose only control of constitutionality is nonjudicial, to those states where this control is pre-eminently judicial, as in the United States. The other states, searching for forms which accord with their philosophies and yet answer the demands of our time, give the best evidence that judicial review is not only a viable but also a most flexible institution.

---

[82] See Brown v. Board of Educ. of Topeka, 347 U.S. 483 (1954); 349 U.S. 294 (1955). For the rise and fall of the "political questions" doctrine as regards legislative reapportionment see SHAPIRO, supra note 4, at 185 ff. The most relevant cases are, of course, Colegrove v. Green, 328 U.S. 549 (1946); and Baker v. Carr, 369 U.S. 186 (1962). See also Kauper, The Supreme Court: Hybrid Organ of State, 21 Sw. L.J. 573-90 (1967).

CHAPTER IV

THE MODERN SYSTEMS OF JUDICIAL REVIEW: THE PROCESS OF CONTROL

§ 1. Two methods of reviewing a constitutional question: "incidenter" and "principaliter"

The differences between the centralized and decentralized systems clearly go far beyond the historical. Largely due to a lack of confidence in the suitability of the traditional judiciary for the new task and to the conviction that judicial review is to a certain extent political in nature, the civil law countries have tended to confine constitutional control to specially created bodies of primarily political appointees. For similar reasons they have also developed different methods of raising and deciding questions of the constitutionality of legislation. Essentially, while the decentralized system encourages private parties to introduce constitutional issues before ordinary tribunals in connection with regular judicial proceedings (review "incidenter"), the centralized approach tends, at least in its archetypal form, to emphasize presentation of constitutional issues before the special constitutional courts via special actions initiated by various government authorities (review "principaliter"). The United States is the country where review "incidenter" is most typical; the Austrian Constitution of 1920, on the other hand, devised a system of review classically "principaliter."[1]

§ 2. The American system as the prototype of decentralized review "incidenter"

In the United States and the other countries—such as Australia, Canada, Japan, Norway, Denmark, and now also Sweden—where similar systems are in force, the question of a law's constitutionality

[1] On the terminology, see for example P. CALAMANDREI, LA ILLEGITTIMITÀ COSTITUZIONALE DELLE LEGGI 5 f. (Padova, Cedam, 1950), republished in 3 OPERE GIURIDICHE 349 f. (M. Cappelletti (ed.), Napoli, Morano, 1968).

cannot be placed before the court "as a principal issue," that is to say in a separate constitutional case instituted ad hoc by a special action.[2] Such questions must form part of a concrete case or controversy (whether civil, penal or any other type), and only arise to the extent that the law under consideration is *relevant* to the decision in the particular case.[3] Thus the court competent to try the case that raises the question of constitutionality will be the very same court which is competent to decide the question itself. Hence matters of constitutional legitimacy of legislation, just as they are not decided by special constitutional courts, so they are not decided by special constitutional procedures. They are *merely incidental* to the case at hand, although sometimes, in view of the general importance of the issue, certain federal or state authorities

---

[2] The possibility that the legislative or executive organs may request advisory opinions on questions of constitutionality from the supreme courts does not represent a derogation of the rule given in the text. Such a practice is found in Canada, India, Norway, Finland and at least ten of the fifty states of the United States. This does not, however, constitute a genuine exercise of judicial review but rather one of constitutional consultation. On this subject, see the comparative study of L. WILDHABER, ADVISORY OPINIONS. RECHTSGUTACHTEN HÖCHSTER GERICHTE (Basel, Helbing & Lichtenhahn, 1962); and see J. BROSSARD, LA COUR SUPRÊME ET LA CONSTITUTION. LE FORUM CONSTITUTIONNEL AU CANADA 145 ff. (Montréal, Les Presses de l'Université de Montréal, 1968); O.P. FIELD, JUDICIAL REVIEW OF LEGISLATION IN TEN SELECTED STATES (Bloomington, University of Indiana Press, 1943); J.A. STORING, NORWEGIAN DEMOCRACY 156 (London, Allen & Unwin, 1963); B.L. STRAYER, JUDICIAL REVIEW OF LEGISLATION IN CANADA 92 f., 182 ff., esp. 201 f., 204 (University of Toronto Press, 1968); Castberg, *Verfassungsgerichtsbarkeit in Norwegen und Dänemark*, in MAX-PLANCK-INSTITUT FÜR AUSLÄNDISCHES ÖFFENTLICHES RECHT UND VÖLKERRECHT, VERFASSUNGSGERICHTSBARKEIT IN DER GEGENWART. LÄNDERBERICHTE UND RECHTSVERGLEICHUNG 425 f. (H. Mosler (ed.), Köln-Berlin, Heymanns, 1962); Edsall, *The Advisory Opinion in North Carolina*, 27 N.C.L. REV. 297-344 (1949); Engelhardt, *Das richterliche Prüfungsrecht im modernen Verfassungsstaat*, 8 JAHRBUCH DES ÖFFENTLICHEN RECHTS DER GEGENWART 117 f. (1959); Field, *The Advisory Opinion—An Analysis*, 24 IND. L.J. 203-30 (1949); Geck, *Judicial Review of Statutes: A Comparative Survey of Present Institutions and Practices*, 51 CORNELL L.Q. 250, 262 ff. (1966); Grant, *Judicial Review in Canada: Procedural Aspects*, 42 CAN. B. REV. 195 ff., esp. 203-14, 221 f. (1964); Saario, *Control of the Constitutionality of Laws in Finland*, 12 AM. J. COMP. L. 194, 197, 198 f. (1963); Thayer, *The Origin and Scope of the American Doctrine of Constitutional Law*, 7 HARV. L. REV. 129, 153 f. (1893).

[3] There has been a recent tendency on the part of the American courts to recognize the existence of a "case or controversy" even before the actual violation of the unconstitutional law by the interested party. The court's action usually takes the form of a preventive declaratory judgment that the challenged statute is unconstitutional, coupled with an injunction against future enforcement of the statute. *See, e.g.,* Epperson v. Arkansas, 393 U.S. 97 (1968); Dombrowski v. Pfister, 380 U.S. 479 (1965); Baggett v. Bullitt, 377 U.S. 360 (1964); Evers v. Dwyer, 358 U.S. 202 (1958) (per curiam); Buchanan v. Batchelor, 308 F. Supp. 729 (N.D. Tex. 1970). Although the claim for a declaratory judgment of unconstitutionality is usually combined with a request for an injunction against enforcement of the law, the Supreme Court has made it clear that the declaratory judgment issue must be considered separately from the conclusions on the propriety of granting an injunction.

may intervene in the proceedings and address to the court what is aptly called an amicus curiae brief, presenting their views on the matter of constitutionality, not as real parties to the action, but rather as interested third parties.[4] As one American scholar has written, American courts, including the Supreme Court, encounter and decide matters of legislative constitutionality "only within the context of concrete adversary litigation" and "only as necessary to the disposition of the case."[5] The same writer further remarks that in the American system, which is undoubtedly the most typical of the systems in which the constitutional jurisdiction is incidental, the matter of constitutionality can be raised in the course of any type of judicial proceeding.[6]

§ 3. The Austrian system of 1920-1929 as the prototype of centralized review "principaliter"

The Austrian system of judicial review in its original form under the *Bundesverfassung* of October 1, 1920, was a direct contrast to the American one, even though it has subsequently been modified. This Constitution not only created a special Constitutional Court—the *Verfassungsgerichtshof*—in which the exclusive competence over matters of constitutionality was centered, but also gave this Court a power of control which could only be exercised after a special plea ("Antrag"). In this way judicial review in Austria, in contrast to the American system, came to be *entirely disassociated from concrete cases* whether civil, penal or administrative. Therefore, while in America judicial review can only be exercised "as an incidental issue" or (as has also been said, even though not entirely accurately) "by way of defense," in Austria it

---

Zwickler v. Koota, 389 U.S. 241, 254 (1967). For similar developments in Australia see G. SAWER, CASES ON THE CONSTITUTION OF THE COMMONWEALTH OF AUSTRALIA 544 ff. (Sydney, The Law Book Co. of Australasia, 3d ed. 1964); McWhinney, *Constitutional Review in the Commonwealth*, in MAX-PLANCK-INSTITUT, *supra* note 2, at 83 f.

[4] *See* Kauper, *Judicial Review of Constitutional Issues in the United States*, in MAX-PLANCK-INSTITUT, *supra* note 2, at 593 f.; J.A.C. GRANT, EL CONTROL JURISDICCIONAL DE LA CONSTITUCIONALIDAD DE LAS LEYES. UNA CONTRIBUCIÓN DE LAS AMÉRICAS A LA CIENCIA POLÍTICA 94-98 (Publicación de la Revista de la Facultad de Derecho de México, 1963); Engelhardt, *supra* note 2, at 122.

[5] Kauper, *supra* note 4, at 571, 573.

[6] *Id.* at 586 f., 634: "The constitutional question, if relevant to the disposition of the case and if asserted by a proper party in interest (plaintiff or defendant) in an adversary proceeding, may be raised regardless of the nature of the proceeding;" such a question can, therefore, "arise in the course of a criminal proceeding, a civil proceeding, a proceeding for damages, for equitable relief, for declaratory judgment or for an extraordinary remedy such as habeas corpus or mandamus."

had to be exercised "as a principal issue" or "by way of action" in a special ad hoc proceeding.

The judges, therefore, under the original Austrian system, with the exception of those in the single Constitutional Court, had no power to review legislation, nor did they have the consequent power not to apply laws which they considered unconstitutional. In effect, this principle was and still is expressly declared by the words of art. 89, para. 1, of the Austrian Constitution: "Review of the validity of duly promulgated laws is not within the powers of the courts." Furthermore, the Austrian judges did not even have the right to ask the Constitutional Court to exercise that review which was forbidden to them. Questions of the constitutionality of laws could be brought before the Constitutional Court only by way of a direct plea by certain political, not judicial, organs mentioned in the Constitution. These organs were the Federal Executive (*Bundesregierung*) for judicial review of laws of the *Länder* (*Landesgesetze*) and the Governments of the *Länder* (*Landesregierungen*) for review of Federal legislation.[7] There was no time limit fixed for the exercise of this right of action by these political organs, which alone possessed the right of access to the Constitutional Court.

§ 4.   Modifications of the Austrian prototype

A glance at the original Austrian system, set up by the 1920 Constitution, shows immediately that it was entirely insufficient. As we have just seen, only the *Länder* and Federal Executives had the right to initiate proceedings for judicial review before the Constitutional Court as a principal issue against federal or *Länder* legislation respectively. Accordingly, review of constitutionality could only have a fairly limited significance. It came, in practice, to be restricted to providing a defense against unconstitutional trespasses on the part of the federal legislature in the sphere of authority reserved to the *Länder* legislatures, and vice-versa. Thus it guaranteed between the federal authorities and the *Länder* a mutual respect for their "constitutional division of competences" (*verfassungsrechtliche Kompetenzverteilung*).[8] On the other hand, laws which curtailed individual liberties remained, practically speaking, outside the ambit of control. Neither the Federal nor the *Länder* Governments were bound to initiate an action for judi-

---

[7] *See* Melichar, *Die Verfassungsgerichtsbarkeit in Österreich*, in MAX-PLANCK-INSTITUT, *supra* note 2, at 442.
   [8] *Id.* at 486.

cial review against laws which they considered unconstitutional. The power was entirely discretionary. And so, inevitably, these political organs felt themselves to be really interested in initiating the action only in fairly rare and exceptional cases. In this way the Constitutional Court could in practice be prevented from the consideration of many unconstitutional laws; and we have already seen how, by virtue of a specific provision of the Constitution, laws, even if manifestly unconstitutional, had to be blindly applied by all the judges as if they were perfectly valid.

An amendment to the Austrian Constitution *(Bundes-Verfassungsnovelle)* in 1929 modified somewhat this system of judicial review exercisable exclusively "by way of action." The current system in Austria is the result of that *Novelle* of 1929, which, though suppressed under the dictatorship,[9] was revived after the last war with but a few variations, which are of no concern for our purposes.

This important constitutional reform of 1929 amended art. 140 of the Austrian Constitution by granting the right held by certain political organs to two ordinary *judicial* organs as well. Thus, the right to initiate proceedings for judicial review before the Constitutional Court was given not only to the Federal and *Länder* Governments, but now also to the *Oberster Gerichtshof* (the highest civil and criminal Court) and to the *Verwaltungsgerichtshof* (the central administrative Court).

There is, however, a difference between the rights of the Federal and *Länder* Governments, and those of these two judicial organs. The latter cannot raise the question of constitutionality before the Constitutional Court "principaliter," *i.e.* by way of direct action. Rather, they do so "incidenter," *i.e.* by way of defense, in the course and on the occasion of a normal case (civil, penal, or administrative) pending before them, where the decision depends on the federal or state law whose constitutionality is in doubt.[10]

The *Novelle* of 1929 thus brought the Austrian system of review a little closer to the American model; and the most obvious improvements over the 1920 Constitution are immediately apparent. While the two highest ordinary courts in Austria are still not them-

---

[9] *See* F. ERMACORA, DER VERFASSUNGSGERICHTSHOF 83 (Graz-Wien-Köln, Verlag Styria, 1956); Ermacora, *Die österreichische Verfassungsgerichtsbarkeit seit 1945,* 8 JAHRBUCH DES ÖFFENTLICHEN RECHTS DER GEGENWART 51 (1959).

[10] *See* art. 140 of the Austrian Constitution ("Der Verfassungsgerichtshof erkennt über Verfassungswidrigkeit eines Bundes- oder Landesgesetzes auf Antrag des Obersten Gerichtshofes oder des Verwaltungsgerichtshofes, sofern ein solches Gesetz die Voraussetzung eines Erkenntnisses des antragstellenden Gerichtshofes bildet. . . .").

selves allowed to perform any functions of control over constitutional legitimacy, they are given the right to ask the Constitutional Court to exercise this control over laws relevant to the decisions in the concrete cases pending before them. This power is no longer discretionary but imposes a real obligation upon the two highest organs of ordinary and administrative justice not to apply laws whose constitutionality is in doubt,[11] without having first heard the binding judgment of the Constitutional Court. Consequently, no law is excluded from the practical possibility of review. It may also be noted that, similar to the amicus curiae, third parties as well as the litigants in the concrete case may intervene before the Constitutional Court. Such an intervention can be made by the interested governments, i.e., the Federal Government in questions concerning the constitutionality of federal laws, or the Government of the *Land* when its law is at issue.[12]

Hence the reform of 1929 notably moderated the most serious defects of the 1920 system, without, however, entirely removing them. It must be emphasized that of all the civil, criminal, and administrative courts, only the two superior Courts have access to the *Verfassungsgerichtshof*. All the other judges must unquestioningly apply the laws to cases coming before them. There is no possibility of their not applying even those laws which appear manifestly unconstitutional. Hence the serious disadvantage results that only in the last stages of a civil, criminal, or administrative case can a law finally be avoided, by being referred to the Constitutional Court by the *Oberster Gerichtshof* or the *Verwaltungsgerichtshof*. Up to that stage, regardless of any manifest unconstitutionality, the inferior judges, as well as governmental agencies, are necessarily bound to apply it.[13]

This most apparent defect of the Austrian system has been avoided both by that of Italy, in effect since 1956, and by that of Germany, adopted by the Bonn Constitution of 1949.[14] This is not, however, to deny the great influence deservedly exercised on both these systems by the ingenious Austrian precedent.

We have already mentioned that both in Germany and Italy, as in Austria, the ordinary judges (civil, criminal, and adminis-

---

[11] See Melichar, *supra* note 7, at 460.
[12] See § 63 of the *Verfassungsgerichtshofgesetz* 1953.
[13] See, e.g., Engelhardt, *supra* note 2, at 114 f., 118 f.
[14] See Friesenhahn, *Die Verfassungsgerichtsbarkeit in der Bundesrepublik Deutschland*, in MAX-PLANCK-INSTITUT, *supra* note 2, at 138.

trative) are forbidden to review the constitutionality of legislation.[15] This function is reserved exclusively to the Constitutional Courts of the respective countries. But in Italy and Germany, contrary to Austria, all the ordinary judges, even the inferior ones, are not passively bound to apply any law which they consider unconstitutional. Rather, they have the power and the duty to place issues of constitutionality before the Constitutional Court so as to obtain a binding decision from that body.[16] Thus, all the judges, and not only those of the superior courts, have the right to invoke the jurisdiction of the Constitutional Court, provided that the law is relevant to the concrete case before them. The case is then suspended until such time as the Constitutional Court shall have decided the preliminary issue of constitutionality.[17]

It is thus apparent that, from the standpoint of the manner in which constitutional issues are presented, the Italian and German systems have drawn considerably closer to the American system of judicial review. It is not the case for Italy and Germany (as it is in the United States) that all the judges are competent to *perform* the function of judicial review. However, they all at least have the right to *require* the Constitutional Court to exercise its powers of review.

Nevertheless, this "incidental" way is not the only method of raising a constitutional issue before the German and Italian Constitutional Courts. Certain political organs have the right to bring a direct action, independent of any concrete case, by instituting an ad hoc proceeding before the Constitutional Court. From this point of view, we see a divergence from the American system on the part of these two European countries, and an approximation to the Austrian system of control of constitutionality.

---

[15] Or, at least, from reviewing the so-called *nachkonstitutionelle Gesetze, i.e.,* post-constitutional legislation. *See id.* at 105 f., 136 f.; Engelhardt, *supra* note 2, at 114. The Italian system does not even have this limitation, according to the important decision No. 1 of the Constitutional Court in 1956 (to be found in 1 GIURISPRUDENZA COSTITUZIONALE 1 (1956)).

[16] *See, e.g.,* Friesenhahn, *supra* note 14, at 136; Sandulli, *Die Verfassungsgerichtsbarkeit in Italien,* in MAX-PLANCK-INSTITUT, *supra* note 2, at 302 f.

[17] *See* art. 1 of the Italian constitutional law of February 9, 1948, No. 1; art. 100, para. 1, of the Bonn Constitution: "Hält ein Gericht ein Gesetz, auf dessen Gültigkeit es bei der Entscheidung ankommt, für verfassungswidrig, so ist das Verfahren auszusetzen und, wenn es sich um die Verletzung der Verfassung eines Landes handelt, die Entscheidung des für Verfassungsstreitigkeiten zuständigen Gerichtes des Landes, wenn es sich um die Verletzung dieses Grundgesetzes handelt, die Entscheidung des Bundesverfassungsgerichtes einzuholen." On this subject see M. CAPPELLETTI, LA PREGIUDIZIALITÀ COSTITUZIONALE NEL PROCESSO CIVILE (Milano, Giuffrè, 1957). German writers speak also of a "Vorfrage"; *see, e.g.,* Engelhardt, *supra* note 2, at 113 ff.

In Italy, this right to convene the Court "by way of direct action" belongs to the executive organs of the regions (giunte regionali) in matters of national or regional laws which a region contends have infringed the area of competence reserved to it by the Constitution (constitutional law of February 9, 1948, No. 1, art. 2). Conversely, this right belongs to the central Executive in disputes over the constitutionality of regional laws (art. 127, para. 4, of the Constitution). In Germany, a still larger selection of institutions and individuals has the right to invoke, "by way of action," the procedures of the Federal Constitutional Court or the Constitutional Courts of the Länder for control of legislation. In particular, this right belongs to the Federal Government, the Governments of the Länder, one third of the members of the Bundestag (art. 93 of the Bonn Constitution),[18] and even to individual citizens if the law tends to the immediate and actual infringement of one of their "fundamental rights."[19]

To sum up, one can say that from the point of view of the processes of control, there was originally a clear distinction between the so-called American approach to judicial review, exercised solely incidentally, and the Austrian system of control exercised solely by way of direct action. This distinction was, however, attenuated in Austria in 1929 and still further in the systems of control adopted in Italy and Germany after the last World War, and recently imitated in certain other countries.[20] Here questions of legislative constitutionality can be brought before the Constitutional Courts in two ways. Firstly, this can be done "incidenter" as a result of the dispute in a concrete case whether civil, criminal, or administrative—one speaks in this context of a konkrete Normenkontrolle (concrete review) or also of an Inzidentkontrolle (incidental control). Secondly, it can be done "principaliter" by means of a direct action brought solely to test the constitutionality of a given law before the Constitutional Court. Here, the initiative will rest either with certain nonjudicial organs, or even with a parliamentary minority or an individual person. For this second method one talks

---

[18] See Friesenhahn, supra note 14, at 133; Engelhardt, supra note 2, at 115.

[19] The Constitution of Bonn did not provide for the right mentioned in the text to be exercisable by individual citizens. This institution (Verfassungsbeschwerde) was set up by the ordinary law of March 12, 1951 on the Bundesverfassungsgericht. See Ch. I, text and notes 67-68 supra.

[20] E.g., in Turkey. See Balta, Die Verfassungsgerichtsbarkeit in der Türkei, in MAX-PLANCK-INSTITUT, supra note 2, at 561-64; Ülkü Azrak, Verfassungsgerichtsbarkeit in der Türkei, 11 JAHRBUCH DES ÖFFENTLICHEN RECHTS DER GEGENWART 73, 86-89 (1962); arts. 149-151 of the Turkish Constitution of 1961.

of *abstrakte Normenkontrolle* (abstract review) so as to show that the review, exercised by the Constitutional Court, is unrelated to any concrete case.[21]

§ 5. Ordinary and extraordinary means of raising constitutional issues in both systems

An examination of the way in which a private party raises a constitutional question in both the centralized and decentralized systems would show both the divergent outlooks as well as the common problems of judicial review in each of the two major western legal families.

In the United States, a private party may raise a constitutional question before any court of first instance, civil or criminal. The court will decide the question along with all others posed by the case. The losing party may then appeal the decisions of first instance and the record of the case will gradually work its way up the judicial hierarchy, the most important issues, including the constitutional, being susceptible to ultimate resolution by the Supreme Court. The constitutional issue is seldom if ever considered apart from the fact situation which gave rise to it.[22]

The process by which a similar constitutional question would be resolved in the civil law countries is quite different. In Italy, for example, the private party—or, for that matter, the court itself *ex officio*—may raise the issue in any stage of any judicial proceeding, but the court is powerless to decide it. Rather, the court simply determines if the issue is relevant to the case and if it is not "manifestly unfounded" (this determination is not appealable, though it may be raised again when the entire case goes before the courts of later instance).[23] Relevance and prima facie foundation being

---

[21] The Mexican system has similarities to the European ones mentioned. Also in Mexico judicial review is not exclusively invoked "by way of action" (as originally in Austria), nor exclusively "incidenter" (as in the United States). The system is mixed or composite, and there is the possibility of an "*acción* de inconstitucionalidad de las leyes" as well as of a "*recurso* de inconstitucionalidad." This last, according to an authoritative analysis of *juicio de amparo,* consists precisely in "un control de constitucionalidad de las leyes *por vía de excepción*." H. FIX ZAMUDIO, EL JUICIO DE AMPARO 179, 251 (México, Porrúa, 1964).

[22] For a detailed analysis of a single constitutional case, from its beginnings in the lower courts to the final resolution in the Supreme Court, and with constant reference to the political factors which surround every constitutional challenge of any importance, see A.F. WESTIN, THE ANATOMY OF A CONSTITUTIONAL LAW CASE (New York, Macmillan, 1958).

[23] *See* M. CAPPELLETTI & J.M. PERILLO, CIVIL PROCEDURE IN ITALY 110 (The Hague, Nijhoff, 1965); CAPPELLETTI, *supra* note 17, at 101 ff., 112 ff.

determined, the issue is referred to the Constitutional Court. However, since the latter cannot decide the other factual and legal issues of the case, these must remain below, to be decided in proceedings which are stayed pending the decision on the constitutional question.[24] This question thus tends to be considered in the abstract and the decision is addressed rather to the statute challenged than to the facts of the case at hand.

A major problem faced by both systems is the avoidance of irreparable injury to the party pending an ultimate decision on the challenged statute. For example, when a person is arbitrarily denied a passport by an administrative agency or when labor union picketers are illegally arrested, the rights denied them are fundamental. If these rights continue to be denied pending vindication in the courts, the harm caused may not be compensable, and the possibility of money damages will be of little comfort. What is needed, then, are special remedies for violations of special rights—remedies which are at once expeditious and which avoid irreparable harm to the aggrieved petitioner pending a final decision.[25]

Both systems have devised such recourses for violations of particularly important rights; these have been partially described.[26] The traditional battery of writs and injunctions available to common law judges has proven effective in precipitating early, if tentative, decisions on constitutional questions. Some of the civil law countries have devised similar statutory remedies for higher law violations; Germany's *Verfassungsbeschwerde* is especially effective in that the Constitutional Court may suspend the application of challenged state actions pending final decision regarding their constitutionality.[27] Italy as yet lacks a similar remedy; the criminal accused must await the making of a formal charge before he may advance his constitutional defense. Similarly, the person denied a fundamental right by an administrative agency must often exhaust irrelevant administrative remedies or build an artificial case *(fictio litis)* before he may go to court and present the ultimately important constitutional question. All of this hearkens back to the old

---

[24] The provisions for staying lower court proceedings are similar in Germany. *See* art. 100 (1) of the Basic Law, and §§ 80-82 of the *Bundesverfassungsgerichtsgesetz*; E. FRIESENHAHN, DIE VERFASSUNGSGERICHTSBARKEIT IN DER BUNDESREPUBLIK DEUTSCHLAND 52 ff. (Köln-Berlin, Heymanns, 1962).

[25] *See* M. CAPPELLETTI, PROCESSO E IDEOLOGIE 531-39 (Bologna, Il Mulino, 1969).

[26] See Ch. I, § 8 *supra*.

[27] *See* § 32 of the *Bundesverfassungsgerichtsgesetz* and references in H. LECHNER, BUNDESVERFASSUNGSGERICHTSGESETZ 196 ff. (München, Beck, 2d ed. 1967).

truth that a right without an adequate remedy is no right at all, and it is to be expected that there will be an increasing recognition in some civil law countries of the inadequacy of the remedial aspect of their new systems of judicial review.[28]

§ 6. The two systems: inherent risks in each

The distinguishing mark of the centralized systems of constitutional control is the lack of a single judicial organ which may consider and resolve all the issues of a particular case. The special constitutional courts are barred from deciding factual disputes, ordinary legal questions, and issues of statutory interpretation; the ordinary courts, in turn, may not decide constitutional challenges.[29]

The results of this lack of any court with complete jurisdiction are profound. First, the ordinary courts are not greatly encouraged to develop a "constitutional consciousness" which would lead them to perform their regular duties (judicial investigations, factual determinations, statutory interpretation, etc.) with an eye to avoiding violations of constitutional rights. The ordinary judge is directly controlled not by the Constitutional Court but by one of the other high courts of his country. None of these latter courts has the formal duty of concerning itself with defining constitutional norms, and the pressures for constitutional awareness are correspondingly less.[30]

---

[28] M. Cappelletti, La giurisdizione costituzionale delle libertà 12 and *passim* (Milano, Giuffrè, 1955); Cappelletti, *supra* note 25, at 531 ff.

[29] "Since the legal authority to interpret statutes lies in the system of ordinary courts, with the Supreme Court of Cassation at its apex, not in the Constitutional Court, the latter body according to the prevailing view does not have the power to combine authoritative interpretation with constitutional judgment." Merryman & Vigoriti, *When Courts Collide: Constitution and Cassation in Italy*, 15 Am. J. Comp. L. 665, 668 (1967). Thus, the typical continental court structure does not resemble the American structure where all courts are subject to the unifying influence of the Supreme Court; rather, there are three or more separate structures, each with its high court. None of the high courts (Cassation, Council of State, Constitutional Court, etc.; see Ch. III, note 61 and accompanying text *supra*) is subject to control by any other court with regard to decisions within its field. For Germany see, however, Ch. V, note 8 *infra*.

[30] An example is afforded by the interpretations given by the ordinary courts, led by the Court of Cassation, in Italy, to various statutes dealing with the criminal accused's right to counsel. These interpretations have "seemed to place a higher value on judicial convenience, economy and expedition than on expansion of the scope of legal protection afforded criminal defendants. . . . One suspects that there may be something self-fulfilling about this. . . . It becomes the primary obligation of the Constitutional Court to translate the precepts of that document [*i.e.* the Constitution] into specific decisions on the constitutionality of statutes. Since that obligation lies principally with the Constitutional Court, other courts can feel free to pursue other principal objectives." Merryman & Vigoriti, *supra* note 29, at 681.

Second, the special constitutional courts inevitably tend to focus not on the particular fact situation in which a given individual was denied a certain right, but rather on the constitutionality of a specified, abstract, statutory proposition. After all, the primary duty of the special constitutional court is not so much to decide a particular case as it is to give a formal declaration of a statute's constitutionality or lack thereof. Since this declaration will bind *erga omnes*, the statute is the matter of concern, not the fact situation which resulted in its being challenged.[31]

Thus, while on the face of it some might say that the centralized system, with review both *incidenter* and by way of direct action, is more complete than its decentralized counterpart,[32] others might claim that the newer form of review suffers from a serious lack of judicial flexibility, largely because of the separation of constitutional questions from specific fact situations. The result may be that the constitutional courts will be unable to avoid deciding questions that would be better postponed, or, worse, they will be unable to perform their duty of protecting individual rights with-

---

[31] "The procedures before the constitutional courts are . . . not adversary, but objective. They do not primarily serve the rights of the parties in the original case, but are to safeguard the legal order regardless of individual interests. . . . The constitutional court's finding regarding the statute is usually more important in its general effect than in its bearing on the original case." Geck, *supra* note 2, at 280 f.

[32] There are various possible fact situations where, despite the apparent certainty of the unconstitutionality, nevertheless no judicial review would be possible simply because of the "incidental nature" of the control current in the United States. Examples are to be found in Kauper, *supra* note 4, at 589 f., 594 f., 606, 609. *See also* H. GALLAND, LE CONTRÔLE JUDICIAIRE DE LA CONSTITUTIONNALITÈ DES LOIS AUX ETATS-UNIS 127 f. (Paris, Sirey, 1932); Cappelletti & Adams, *Judicial Review of Legislation: European Antecedents and Adaptations,* 79 HARV. L. REV. 1207, 1221 (1966): "The American system—which considers 'nonjusticiable' any constitutional question not arising from a concrete case—in practice denies a citizen the right to his day in court whenever the cost and inconvenience involved in disobeying a law and fighting it through the courts are too great." Note, however, what has been said in note 3 *supra.* A Japanese writer has referred to similar limitations which are appearing in Japan, where, as noted, the American system was adopted after the last war. Kiyomiya, *Verfassungsgerichtsbarkeit in Japan,* in MAX-PLANCK-INSTITUT, *supra* note 2, at 329 f. *See also* M. MAKI, COURT AND CONSTITUTION IN JAPAN. SELECTED SUPREME COURT DECISIONS 1948-60, at 328 ff., 362 ff. (Seattle, University of Washington Press, 1964); von Mehren, in LAW IN JAPAN: THE LEGAL ORDER IN A CHANGING SOCIETY 422 (A.T. von Mehren (ed.), Cambridge, Mass., Harvard University Press, 1963); Hayashida, *Constitutional Court and Supreme Court of Japan,* in 2 DIE MODERNE DEMOKRATIE UND IHR RECHT. FESTSCHRIFT FÜR GERHARD LEIBHOLZ ZUM 65. GEBURTSTAG 423 (Tübingen, Mohr, 1966).

out provoking dangerous conflicts with other branches of government.[33]

The ability to say not "yes" or "no," but rather "maybe" to a constitutional question is a hallmark of the American Supreme Court, which has evolved an impressive array of means of avoiding delicate constitutional questions. The Court, to insure that it is not flooded with questions to which it cannot give adequate attention, or to put off a decision of great delicacy, will require that the question posed arise from a real, not a feigned, dispute, that it have been timely put and debated in the lower courts, and that the interest of the parties involved be such as to insure an adequate presentation of all points of view.[34]

The Court may not always apply these and similar doctrines neutrally. It may in fact use them to tip the judicial scales for or against the constitutional challenge, *without* a formal declaration of constitutionality or unconstitutionality. Perhaps because of their youth, or perhaps due to the structural features outlined above, the European courts have not yet gone as far in developing methods of blocking the legislature without provoking dangerous reactions.

What is this "mediating way between the ultimates of legitimation and invalidation"?[35] One aspect is the use of the Court's power to interpret statutes so as to avoid any construction which could be conceived of as unconstitutional. Or the Court might say that a given statute, if it is to limit a certain right, must do so explicitly or be voided for vagueness. Or it could be affirmed that while Congress might be able to legislate in a given field, it must not dele-

---

[33] See the prophetic insights of A. DE TOCQUEVILLE, 1 DE LA DÉMO-CRATIE EN AMÉRIQUE, Ch. VI, at 181-83 (Bruxelles, Méline, Cans et Co., 1840). The French writer admitted that the American system of control was incomplete and not without disadvantages ("la censure judiciaire, exercée par les tribunaux sur la législation, ne peut s'étendre sans distinction à toutes les lois, car il en est qui ne peuvent jamais donner lieu à cette sorte de contestation nettement formulée, qu'on nomme un procès. Et, lorsqu'une pareille contestation est possible, on peut encore concevoir qu'il ne se rencontre personne qui veuille en saisir les tribunaux"); however, he considered that precisely because of this incompleteness, the American system was less dangerous ("les Américains ont souvent senti cet inconvénient, mais ils ont laissé le remède incomplet, de peur de lui donner . . . une efficacité dangereuse").

[34] See generally H.J. ABRAHAM, THE JUDICIAL PROCESS 355-77 (New York, Oxford University Press, 2d ed. 1968).

[35] A.M. BICKEL, THE LEAST DANGEROUS BRANCH 132 (Indianapolis-New York, Bobbs-Merrill, 1962).

gate this power to non-elective administrative bodies.[36] In all these cases—the reinterpreted statute, the statute voided for vagueness, and the law struck down for having improperly delegated a particular power—the Court effectively protects the right of the person challenging the law, but does so without formally declaring that a given norm may not be established by the legislature. In all of these cases the legislature is not barred from reconsidering the statute and re-enacting it in such a way as to make clear its desire to pass the law, but political reality being what it is, the legislature often finds it impracticable to do so.

Whether the special constitutional courts may be able to evolve similar weapons of limited warfare against unconstitutionality is open to question. What is clear is the difficulty of doing so, in light of their lack of the formal power to interpret statutes[37] and to

---

[36] The "vagueness" standard has been applied either neutrally or with intent to restrain the legislature. When applied neutrally, the standard may refer to the duty to give "fair warning" to the person who plans his acts with reference to the text of the law, and also to the need to avoid giving uncontrolled discretion to the nonelected officials who, in the end, give content to the vague law. When speaking of Congressional investigations, on the other hand, the Court made it clear that this quintessentially Congressional function was being exercised so as to threaten first amendment liberties; the authorizing statute was vague in that it seemed not to have taken sufficient account of this. *See* BICKEL, *supra* note 35, at 150-60.

The doctrine of nondelegability, on the other hand, has been considerably diluted. While the cases establishing the doctrine have never been overruled, no practical limit has been placed on congressional power to delegate authority. Frank, *The United States Supreme Court, 1947-1948*, 16 U. CHI. L. REV. 1, 16 (1948).

[37] When a constitutional court takes it upon itself to interpret a statute so as to avoid a conflict with higher constitutional standards, it runs a serious risk of conflict with the highest ordinary courts, which claim complete independence from the constitutional court in matters of statutory interpretation. *See* Merryman & Vigoriti, *supra* note 29; for Germany, however, see Ch. V, note 8 *infra*. On the role of interpretation in the jurisprudence of the constitutional courts see generally E. FORSTHOFF, ZUR PROBLEMATIK DER VERFASSUNGSAUSLEGUNG (Stuttgart, Kohlhammer, 1961); V. HAAK, NORMENKONTROLLE UND VERFASSUNGSKONFORME GESETZESAUSLEGUNG DES RICHTERS (Bonn, Röhrscheid, 1963); Ascarelli, *Giurisprudenza costituzionale e teoria dell'interpretazione*, 12 RIVISTA DI DIRITTO PROCESSUALE 351 ff. (1967); Pierandrei, *Prinzipien der Verfassungsinterpretation in Italien*, 12 JAHRBUCH DES ÖFFENTLICHEN RECHTS DER GEGENWART 201 ff. (1963).

It should not be ignored that there are signs of attempts by the constitutional courts in the civil law countries to develop their own sort of flexibility. The German Constitutional Court, for example, has its own version of the "political question" doctrine. *See* H. LAUFER, VERFASSUNGSGERICHTSBARKEIT UND POLITISCHER PROZESS 379 ff., esp. 419 (Tübingen, Mohr, 1968). The Italian Constitutional Court may have an efficacious tool in its ability to uphold, without *erga omnes* effect, the constitutionality of a law. Thus a statute, upheld in one case, may be reconsidered later without any prejudice to the Court's ability to find it invalid. Cappelletti, *Pronunce di rigetto nel processo costituzionale delle libertà e cosa giudicata*, 11 (pt. 1) RIVISTA DI DIRITTO PROCESSUALE 135 ff. (1956).

refuse jurisdiction for purely discretionary reasons, and in view of their tendency to consider constitutional issues in the abstract.[38]

The advisability of conferring such broad powers on the constitutional courts is quite another matter. The United States Supreme Court has often used its "political question," "case and controversy" and "standing" doctrines to delay decisions on statutes which may, in the meantime, cause great hardship to those affected. Indeed the cost and inconvenience of mounting a constitutional case may be such that decades may pass before a plaintiff is found who is willing, for example, to violate the statute, submit to arrest, and then go through the long process of litigation which leads to a hearing before the Supreme Court.[39]

Indeed, the latitude given the American Supreme Court is at once an expression of confidence in the judiciary and a realization that "judicial review is at least potentially a deviant institution in a democratic society."[40] On the one hand there is faith that the judiciary will not use its tools unscrupulously to deny hearings indefinitely to those who deserve them. At the same time, the courts have seen that since their effectiveness rests on the esteem in which they are held by the electorate, they must always keep in mind the attitudes of that electorate. Certain questions are too explosive to be decided by any judicial body; *Dred Scott* presented such a case. Other questions should be delayed, or referred back to the legislature for a more considered opinion; many of the national security cases are examples.[41] It is paradoxical that judicial review in Europe, where there has always been an extreme concern with the political implications of judicial control of legislation, seems to encourage politically dangerous decisions by the judges called upon to administer it.

---

[38] Note the existence of a similar sort of review in the abstract by the U.S. Supreme Court. The Judicial Code provides that the various courts of appeal may certify "any question of law in any civil or criminal case" to the Supreme Court *for binding instructions.* The latter then may decide whether to consider singly the question posed or whether to request that the whole case be sent up for resolution. In fact, the process of certification is very seldom used. *See* 28 U.S.C. 1254 (1964); Taylor v. Atlantic Maritime Company, 181 F.2d 84 (2d Cir. 1950).

[39] A classic example is the Connecticut birth control statute which was not declared unconstitutional until 1965 though there had been challenges made as early as 1943. Each time before 1965, when the question was brought before the Court, it was avoided through the invocation of devices similar to those described in the text. *See* BICKEL, *supra* note 35, at 143-56.

[40] *Id.* at 128.

[41] *See id.* at 164-69.

§ 7. Converging trends

Yet it again behooves us, after contrasting the two systems of judicial review, to emphasize their growing similarities. The European prototype—one single court vested with the power to entertain constitutional questions brought *principaliter* and abstracted from concrete cases—is, as has been shown, far removed from the systems now in force in Italy and Germany, and, to an extent, in Austria itself, where the lower courts may play a real part in judicial review, incidentally to their function of adjudicating ordinary cases.

Similarly in the United States, the Marshall reasoning, with its emphasis on the incidental nature of judicial review, seems somewhat at variance with the recent evolution of the institution. The old maxims of judicial restraint—"case and controversy," "justiciability," "standing," etc.—have been diluted by the Court's acceptance of class actions, requests for declaratory relief, and other means of raising constitutional issues which are only technically in accord with the requirements of concrete litigation. The Supreme Court, by accepting in this way questions once not amenable to review, and by using certiorari to shunt aside nonconstitutional questions, seems to have realized its hybrid nature. It is only in some ways an ordinary court of appeals; in others it is, like the European constitutional courts, "a special organ of constitutional review."[42]

We are, of course, speaking of the United States Supreme Court under Chief Justice Warren.[43] The most distinctive feature of judicial review in America is its ambiguity. Recent developments have not taken from the Court its tools for exercising discretion. While these tools have recently been used to open wide the doors to liberal constitutional interpretations, they may also, in the hands of a Court influenced by different times and personalities, be used to effect a return to more traditional ways.

---

[42] Kauper, *The Supreme Court: Hybrid Organ of State*, 21 Sw. L.J. 573, 577 (1967). "We are accepting the notion that the Court is the guardian of the Constitution and that we should not tolerate roadblocks standing in the way of the Court's opportunity to decide constitutional issues. As we progress with this idea the old notion that the power to pass on constitutional questions is simply incident to the power to dispose of a concrete case loses much of its substance." *Id.* See Ch. III, text and notes 58, 81 *supra*.

[43] *See generally* A.M. BICKEL, POLITICS AND THE WARREN COURT (New York, Harper & Row, 1965); A.M. BICKEL, THE SUPREME COURT AND THE IDEA OF PROGRESS (New York, Harper & Row, 1970); A. COX, THE WARREN COURT, CONSTITUTIONAL DECISION AS AN INSTRUMENT OF REFORM (Cambridge, Harvard University Press, 1968); Black, *The Unfinished Business of the Warren Court*, 46 WASH. L. REV. 3 (1970).

CHAPTER V

THE MODERN SYSTEMS OF JUDICIAL REVIEW: THE EFFECTS OF CONTROL

§ 1. Effects of control: theory and reality

The dilemmas posed by judicial review in a democracy are perhaps nowhere more apparent than when one speaks of the effects of a decision that a state action is unconstitutional. Is the statute involved to be voided in part or in its entirety? Is the decision to bind all future litigants or only those immediately before the court? Is the newly defined constitutional right to be applied retroactively or prospectively? Behind the terse questions lies a mass of issues, subtle and complicated, for which all attempts at broad theoretical explanations have been inadequate. So while both the centralized and decentralized systems of review offer, in their theoretical bases, widely divergent answers to the questions posed, practical considerations in each system have caused a striking convergence between them.

§ 2. Decisions: "inter partes" or "erga omnes"?

Austria's Constitutional Court, again the archetype of the centralized systems, makes its decisions binding not only on the parties to the case, but also on all others finding themselves similarly situated in the future. Thus, a decision of unconstitutionality gives rise to an annulment which, although not retroactive, yet operates *erga omnes*. Hence one speaks appropriately of an "Allgemeinwirkung" or general efficacy. The law, in other words, once a judgment of unconstitutionality has been given, is invalidated for everyone, just as if it had been abrogated by a subsequent statute; and the legislative enactments which preceded the unconstitutional one return into force (art. 140, § 4, of the Austrian Constitution), unless the Constitutional Court decrees otherwise.

The American system is based on a quite opposite theory,[1] as are those systems, such as the Japanese one, which have modeled themselves upon it.[2] The same can be said even for some more original systems, such as the Mexican one where the "principio de la relatividad," corresponding to the so-called "fórmula de Otero," prevails.[3] The fundamental rule in all these systems is that the judge must not go beyond nonapplication of the law in the particular case. Thus judicial review does not have, as in Austria, Italy, Germany and elsewhere, general *erga omnes* efficacy, but only a special *inter partes* validity, related solely to the concrete case ("Individualwirkung"). This element, however, has largely been eliminated in the United States by force of the principle of stare decisis,[4] especially where there is a decision of the Supreme Court. Even in Mexico, it has been considerably attenuated, if not eliminated, through the limited binding force accorded to the "jurisprudencia" of the *Suprema Corte de Justicia,* as well as through the institution of the *suplencia de la queja deficiente* introduced in 1951.[5]

The refusal of the United States Supreme Court to make formal, permanently binding decrees of unconstitutionality is partly based on myth, and partly on a deeply felt need to relate judicial decisions to present realities and not to future possibilities. On one hand, it is felt that open declarations of permanent nullity, declarations at times accompanied by a recital of previous laws, once

---

[1] "In a strict sense, a decision on a constitutional question has relevancy only for the parties to the case." Kauper, *Judicial Review of Constitutional Issues in the United States,* in MAX-PLANCK-INSTITUT FÜR AUSLÄNDISCHES ÖFFENTLICHES RECHT UND VÖLKERRECHT, VERFASSUNGSGERICHTSBARKEIT IN DER GEGENWART. LÄNDERBERICHTE UND RECHTSVERGLEICHUNG 611 (H. Mosler (ed.), Köln-Berlin, Heymanns, 1962). *See also* W.J. WAGNER, THE FEDERAL STATES AND THEIR JUDICIARY (A COMPARATIVE STUDY IN CONSTITUTIONAL LAW AND ORGANIZATION OF COURTS IN FEDERAL STATES) 103 n.100 (The Hague, Mouton, 1959).

[2] *See* Kiyomiya, *Verfassungsgerichtsbarkeit in Japan,* in MAX-PLANCK-INSTITUT, *supra* note 1, at 334.

[3] Art. 107, § 2, of the Mexican Federal Constitution and art. 76 of the *Ley orgánica de amparo,* under which the judgment can never "make a general declaration respecting the statute or act which gave rise to it"; *see, e.g.,* H. FIX ZAMUDIO, EL JUICIO DE AMPARO 188 ff., 378 f., 400 (México, Porrúa, 1964).

[4] Thus in one of the desegregation cases, Mr. Justice Frankfurter could state that Arkansas was "legally and morally before the Court," although not a formal party. The Justice stated that the Court's interpretations of the Constitution must be obeyed by everyone, rather than only by the parties to the case. Cooper v. Aaron, 358 U.S. 1, 22, 24 (1958) (Frankfurter, J., concurring). *See* Kauper, *supra* note 1, at 611; WAGNER, *supra* note 1, at 103 n.100.

[5] *See* Ch. III, note 35 *supra;* FIX ZAMUDIO, *supra* note 3, at 189 ff., 296-301, 403 f., 406-08.

superseded but given new force, smack far too much of judicial law-making. It is certainly a myth that judges never make law, but only declare it, yet this myth is at the basis of popular acceptance of judicial review in the United States and, according to many, it should not be lightly disregarded.[6] On a more practical plane, there is a realization that no judge can foresee all the possible applications of a given statute, and that no judge, therefore, should be asked to do so. "There are sound reasons, grounded not only in theory but in the judicial experience of centuries . . . for believing that the hard, confining, and yet enlarging context of a real controversy leads to sounder and more enduring judgments. 'Every tendency to deal with constitutional questions abstractly,' Professor Felix Frankfurter wrote a generation ago, 'to formulate them in terms of barren legal questions, leads to dialectics, to sterile conclusions unrelated to actualities.' "[7]

But all this says more about past attitudes than about present reality. The judges of the centralized courts appear more and more to share with their American counterparts a realization of the frequent need to limit the future effects of their decisions. They often try to evade sweeping declarations of constitutionality both by interpreting statutes to avoid constitutional problems, and, if this proves impossible, by excising from the statute only the most offensive parts and leaving the rest as an effective statement of the legislative will. The choices made by the judges—whether to reinterpret, to totally invalidate, or to save part of the law—are often made in both systems not only by reference to plain texts, but also to "motives of political or social seasonableness."[8]

---

[6] See generally Mishkin, *The High Court, the Great Writ, and the Due Process of Time and Law*, 79 HARV. L. REV. 56, 58-66 (1965). While generally approving of the United States Supreme Court's pragmatic approach to questions of effects of constitutional judgments, Mishkin is leery of the claim that the Court has a general power to delimit the effects of any of its decisions as it chooses, since such discretion would be exercised with reference to factors more political than judicial.

[7] A.M. BICKEL, THE LEAST DANGEROUS BRANCH 115 f. (Indianapolis-New York, Bobbs-Merrill, 1962).

[8] Branca, *L'illegittimità parziale nelle sentenze della corte costituzionale*, in LA GIUSTIZIA COSTITUZIONALE 68 (G. Maranini (ed.), Firenze, Vallecchi, 1966). Note that in Italy, at least, the device of interpreting the statute so as to avoid the constitutional question (*i.e.* supplying an *interpretazione adeguatrice*) is weakened by the fact that the interpretations, as opposed to decisions of unconstitutionality, of the law by the Constitutional Court are not binding on the ordinary courts which look rather to the Court of Cassation for guidance on such questions. See Ch. IV, note 29 and accompanying text *supra*. The problem is somewhat less pressing in Germany due to the existence of a statute saying that pronouncements of the Constitutional Court, *including interpretations*, which grow out of constitutional cases, bind the lower courts. See *Bundesverfassungsgerichtsgesetz*, § 31(1).

The United States Supreme Court has, in turn, been forced, by the very weightiness of recent questions brought before it, to take account of the legislative implications of its function, and to frame its decrees with regard for their *erga omnes* effects. The school segregation and voter reapportionment cases were, for example, class actions, *i.e.*, they asked relief not only for the individual plaintiffs concerned, but for "all others similarly situated."[9] By its nature the class action asks for more than *inter partes* relief; it takes away the cushioning effects provided by the fact that the significance of traditional constitutional cases was felt only gradually as successive individual litigants sought to vindicate their newly defined rights. There were few areas where the Court sensed greater dangers than in those of racial integration and legislative redistricting. Once having decided to reach these constitutional questions, therefore, the Court had little choice but to frame decrees strikingly legislative in nature. The original segregation cases were given future applicability only; until *Alexander v. Board of Education*,[10] the schools were to be desegregated not forthwith, but "with all deliberate speed." Reapportionment cases are often similarly legislative and future oriented.[11] This is far beyond mere settlement of disputes between private parties.

§ 3.   Decisions: retroactive or prospective?

Here again both systems of judicial review have moved far beyond their original premises.

In the decentralized systems, according to more traditional concepts, an unconstitutional law, being contrary to a superior norm, is held to be absolutely null and void. Hence, we can see that the judge, in the exercise of his power of review, does not annul but merely declares the pre-existing nullity of the unconstitutional law.[12]

---

[9] *See* Baker v. Carr, 369 U.S. 186 (1962), and Brown v. Board of Education, 347 U.S. 483 (1954).

Public actions are another example of an area where the requirement of concreteness is attenuated. L.L. JAFFE, JUDICIAL CONTROL OF ADMINISTRATIVE ACTION 459-500 (Boston, Little, Brown, 1965).

[10] 396 U.S. 19 (1969).

[11] Take, for example, Reynolds v. Sims, 377 U.S. 533 (1964), where the Supreme Court praised the lower court for having instituted its own reapportionment plan for an upcoming election, pending the time when the legislature should devise a scheme which would meet the court's approval.

[12] *See* E.S. CORWIN, THE "HIGHER LAW" BACKGROUND OF AMERICAN CONSTITUTIONAL LAW 14 (Ithaca, N.Y., Cornell University Press, 1955, fifth printing, 1963), published in 42 HARV. L. REV. 149 (1928) ("unconstitutional statutes are unconstitutional *per se,* and not because of any authority attaching to

In the Austrian system, on the other hand, an unconstitutional law is not void, but merely voidable; even if unconstitutional, such a law is valid and effective up to the moment when the decision of the Constitutional Court is published. The Austrian Constitutional Court, therefore, does not merely declare a pre-existing nullity, but it annuls and quashes ("aufhebt") the unconstitutional law. And this is not all. What is even more remarkable is that the Austrian Constitutional Court has a discretionary power to order that the annulment of the law shall only operate from a fixed date subsequent to the publication ("Kundmachung") of its judgment, provided that the deferment of the constitutive (i.e., annulling) effect of the judgment should not be for more than one year.[13] Incidentally one might also mention that this last provision has been followed by the recent Turkish Constitution, although with the limitation that the effective date of the Constitutional Court's decision shall be deferred for no more than six months. A similar provision is also to be found in the Yugoslav system adopted in 1963.[14]

the court that so pronounces them"). *Id.* at 48 ("when the Supreme Court of the United States pronounces an act of Congress 'void', it ordinarily means void *ab initio*, because beyond the power of Congress to enact"). *Id.*, at 33, 49, 55, 77. *See also* J.A.C. GRANT, EL CONTROL JURISDICCIONAL DE LA CONSTITUCIONALIDAD DE LAS LEYES. UNA CONTRIBUCIÓN DE LAS AMÉRICAS A LA CIENCIA POLÍTICA 40 ff. (Publicación de la Revista de la Facultad de Derecho de México, 1963), with other references. The same is true for Canada and Australia: *see* J. BROSSARD, LA COUR SUPRÊME ET LA CONSTITUTION. LE FORUM CONSTITUTIONNEL AU CANADA 70, 151 (Montréal, Les Presses de l'Université de Montréal, 1968).

[13] *See* art. 140, § 3, of the Austrian Constitution: ". . . die Aufhebung tritt am Tage der Kundmachung in Kraft, wenn nicht der Verfassungsgerichtshof für das Ausserkrafttreten eine Frist bestimmt. Diese Frist darf ein Jahr nicht überschreiten." Note, however, that even when the Austrian Constitutional Court chooses to defer the general effect of a decision of unconstitutionality, the parties to the original case in which the issue was raised and decided *will* have the benefits of the declaration of unconstitutionality. *See* F. ERMACORA, DER VERFASSUNGSGERICHTSHOF 262 (Graz-Wien-Köln, Verlag Styria, 1956); L. WERNER & H. KLECATSKY, DAS ÖSTERREICHISCHE BUNDESVERFASSUNGSRECHT 263 (Wien, Manz, 1961).

[14] For the Turkish Republic *see* the Constitution of July 9, 1961, art. 152, para. 2; *see also* Balta, *Die Verfassungsgerichtsbarkeit in der Türkei*, in MAX-PLANCK-INSTITUT, *supra* note 1, at 564; Ülkü Azrak, *Verfassungsgerichtsbarkeit in der Türkei*, 11 JAHRBUCH DES ÖFFENTLICHEN RECHTS DER GEGENWART 89 (1962).

For Yugoslavia *see* arts. 245 and 246 of the Constitution of 1963. If the Yugoslav Federal Constitutional Court declares a federal law to be contrary to the Federal Constitution, the Federal Parliament is obliged to adapt the law to the Constitution within six months. The same time limit of six months applies to the Parliaments of the Federate Republics for their obligation to adapt to the Federal Constitution state laws which the Constitutional Court has declared unconstitutional. In both instances, the law ceases to have any force at all if action is not taken within the time limit. *See* Rozmaryn, *La Constitution, loi fondamentale de l'Etat socialiste*, in P. BISCARETTI DI RUFFÌA & S. ROZMARYN, LA CONSTITUTION COMME LOI FONDAMENTALE DANS LES ETATS DE L'EUROPE OCCIDENTALE ET DANS LES ETATS SOCIALISTES 111 (Torino & Paris, Giappichelli & Librairie Générale de Droit et de Jurisprudence, 1966).

To sum up, the American system of judicial review has the character of a merely "declaratory" review. At any rate this is the traditional view, although lately it has been the subject of much discussion and modification as we shall see. The Austrian system, on the other hand, has taken the form of review "constitutive" of the invalidity and hence of the ineffectiveness of the law in opposition to the Constitution. As a logical result, in the former system the judgment operates *ex tunc*, retroactively, for it is a simple ascertainment of a pre-existing nullity.[15] In the Austrian system, on the contrary, the judgment of unconstitutionality, being constitutive, operates *ex nunc* or even *pro futuro*, without any retroactive effect.[16]

Italy and Germany are again, in a sense, half-way between the more "concrete," pragmatic American approach, tied to the immediate requirements of individual cases, and that more theoretical, abstract and "general" one followed in Kelsen's Austrian system. Both in Italy and in Germany the judgment, in which the Constitutional Court pronounces the unconstitutionality of a law, has validity *erga omnes*, "Allgemeinwirkung," just as in Austria. Hence the unconstitutional law is invalidated for everyone and for always, and not merely denied application in the concrete case. However, both in Italy and in Germany—and in the latter country even more definitely than in the former—it is not accepted that the judgment of unconstitutionality be effective only *ex nunc* or *pro futuro*. Rather, the efficacy in principle operates retroactively *(ex tunc)*.

In other words, both in Italy and Germany—as in the United States—the mere fact of unconstitutionality is a ground of absolute nullity and therefore of ineffectiveness *ipso jure* of the laws, even

---

Rules regarding the effects of decisions of unconstitutionality in Cyprus are quite complex: a law challenged because of its discrimination against a nationality group may be annulled only prospectively; if the question regards a conflict of competence between governmental authorities, the court decides whether the decision has effect *ab initio* or only from the date when the conflict of competence arose. Finally, if the constitutional question has arisen through party initiative in the course of ordinary litigation, the decision *may not* bind any but the parties to the case at hand. *See* arts. 137-144 of the Cypriot Constitution, and Ch. III, notes 18, 55 *supra*. *See* Geck, *Judicial Review of Statutes: A Comparative Survey of Present Institutions and Practices,* 51 CORNELL L.Q. 250, 282 (1966).

[15] *See, e.g.,* WAGNER, *supra* note 1, at 102: "As a matter of principle, the declaration of unconstitutionality has a retroactive character, as the challenged statute was bad at its very inception." *But cf.* in this section (a-c) *infra.*

[16] Note again art. 140, § 3, of the Austrian Constitution (note 13 *supra*). *See* ERMACORA, *supra* note 13, at 260 ff.

before the actual unconstitutionality has been solemnly declared in the binding judgment of the Constitutional Court.[17]

The Italian and German departures from the Austrian model may give some indication of the abandonment, by both systems of review, of a purely theoretical approach to the retroactivity problem. Instead, judicial review everywhere is influenced by practical considerations, among which are:

a) *The need to reward the plaintiff who brings his constitutional complaint before the courts:* As previously noted, the Austrian *Bundes-Verfassungsnovelle* of 1929 amended the Constitution and gave the two Austrian superior courts, the *Oberster Gerichtshof* and the *Verwaltungsgerichtshof*, the right to raise constitutional issues before the Constitutional Court, limited to the laws relevant to the particular case being heard by them. But how could this new right be reconciled with the notion of the constitutive validity of the Constitutional Court's judgment operating not retroactively but only *ex nunc* or *pro futuro?*

The question needs clarification. One should consider that in lawsuits (civil, criminal, or administrative) coming before the courts, the issue is always one of rights, duties, status, and responsibilities arising from facts having occurred in the past. These facts—contracts, torts, transfers of land, etc.—are governed by a legal norm valid at the moment they arise (and therefore at a time anterior to the judicial proceeding). Let us now take the hypothesis of the unconstitutionality of that legal norm. Under the American system (according to the traditional interpretation) and likewise in modern Italy and Germany, that norm, being unconstitutional, was invalid even before it was actually declared unconstitutional through the instrument of judicial review. Therefore it

---

[17] *See* Friesenhahn, *Die Verfassungsgerichtsbarkeit in der Bundesrepublik Deutschland,* in MAX-PLANCK-INSTITUT, *supra* note 1, at 135, 142 f.; Sandulli, *Die Verfassungsgerichtsbarkeit in Italien,* in *id.* at 307 f. *See also* H. LECHNER, BUNDESVERFASSUNGSGERICHTSGESETZ 280 (München, Beck, 2d ed. 1967); Engelhardt, *Das richterliche Prüfungsrecht im modernen Verfassungsstaat,* 8 JAHRBUCH DES ÖFFENTLICHEN RECHTS DER GEGENWART 133 (1959). *But see* C. BÖCKENFÖRDE, DIE SOGENANNTE NICHTIGKEIT VERFASSUNGSWIDRIGER GESETZE (Berlin, Duncker & Humblot, 1966); Esposito, *Il controllo giurisdizionale sulla costituzionalità delle leggi in Italia,* 5 (pt. 1) RIVISTA DI DIRITTO PROCESSUALE 296-98 (1950). On the retroactive effect of decisions of unconstitutionality issuing from the Italian Constitutional Court see the judgment of the Court, No. 127 of December 29, 1966, 22 RIVISTA DI DIRITTO PROCESSUALE 128 ff. (1967) with comments by E.T. Liebman; on the same lines, although with an unacceptable limitation much criticised by academic thought, see also the judgment of the Italian Court of Cassation, United Criminal Sections, December 11, 1965, 21 RIVISTA DI DIRITTO PROCESSUALE 118 ff. (1966) with comments by L. Bianchi d'Espinosa.

was invalid even in respect to facts taking place before the judicial control of constitutionality was exercised. Under the Austrian system, on the other hand, the unconstitutional norm is held perfectly valid and effective at least up to the moment when the decision of the Constitutional Court, lacking retroactive force, is published. In this way, the events, which are the object of the case pending before the *Oberster Gerichtshof* or the *Verwaltungsgerichtshof*, were—at the time of their occurrence—validly and effectively governed by the unconstitutional norm. The following result would therefore be perfectly logical and coherent in theory, although just as absurd and unacceptable in practice: the decision of the Constitutional Court should not have any effect upon the very case pending before the *Oberster Gerichtshof* or the *Verwaltungsgerichtshof* in the course of which the question of constitutionality arose.[18]

Precisely in order to avoid this absurd consequence, the Austrian system, as it was after the reform of 1929 and as it is today, has admitted a partial modification of the idea rigorously adhered to in 1920, which denied any retroactivity at all to the decisions of the Constitutional Court. The reformed system of 1929 has in fact accepted that—limited to the concrete case in which the issue of constitutionality has arisen "incidenter"—the law declared unconstitutional by the Constitutional Court should not be applied to events taking place prior to the judgment itself.[19] Kelsen himself, writing in 1929, had to recognize that "the retroactive effect of the annulment is a technical necessity since, without it, the [judicial] authorities having to apply the law would have no immediate and therefore no sufficiently strong interest to put the machinery of the Constitutional Court in motion . . . . They must be encouraged to submit these claims by giving a retroactive effect to the annul-

---

[18] An example of the absurd, and even unjust, consequence of a strict adherence to the theory of the constitutive nonretroactive effect of judgments might be the following: a plaintiff brings an action against the state authorities, who have levied an estate tax against him, claiming that the Constitution forbids the levying of estate taxes. Even if the Constitutional Court upholds his claim, the plaintiff will nevertheless be bound to pay, for his obligation to pay preceded the Court's judgment, *i.e.* arose when the unconstitutional law was still valid.

[19] *See* ERMACORA, *supra* note 13, at 260; Melichar, *Die Verfassungsgerichtsbarkeit in Österreich*, in MAX-PLANCK-INSTITUT, *supra* note 1, at 463 ("im Falle der Inzidentkontrolle wirkt die Aufhebung aber auf die Rechtssache zurück, die Anlass zur Einleitung des Gesetzesprüfungsverfahrens gegeben hat. Alle übrigen, bis zum Inkrafttreten der Aufhebung gesetzten Vollzugsakte der Verwaltung und der Gerichte werden durch die Aufhebung nicht berührt"); Engelhardt, *supra* note 17, at 134; Geck, *supra* note 14, at 283 f.; note 13 *supra*.

ment in the concrete case."[20] However, the retroactive application of the decision to only the parties of the case at hand and not to all others similarly situated can obviously result in serious inequality.

b) *The reliance factor:* As practical necessity in Austria required the modification of the strict theory of nonretroactivity in 1929, similarly in the United States, as in Germany and Italy, a parallel necessity has compelled considerable modification of the opposite doctrine of *ex tunc* efficacy, or retroactivity. This doctrine presupposes that the unconstitutional law is null and void *ab origine*. This means that every act—whether private, *e.g.*, a contract, or public, *e.g.*, an administrative act or judicial decision—will have no valid legal basis if it is performed on the strength of the unconstitutional law. It can happen, however, that an unconstitutional law may have been generally and unquestioningly applied by public bodies and private citizens for a considerable time. For example, an office-holder, elected or nominated on the basis of a law declared unconstitutional at a much later date, may have held that office for a long period; the state may have levied a tax for many years, or a private citizen drawn a pension or performed certain contractual obligations, on the basis of a law which subsequently turns out to be unconstitutional; and so one might go on with endless examples. What then happens with a law which, after being unquestioningly applied for many years, is at some time held unconstitutional in a judgment having retroactive effects according to the doctrine presented here? Is it possible to abolish all the effects which have resulted, without any valid legal basis, from those public and private acts which formerly were done in accordance with such a law?

The answer to these questions has been inspired, especially in the case law of the American courts, by the development of a pragmatic and broad-minded way of thinking[21] which, it is submitted, has on the whole ably risen to the occasion. There has also

---

[20] Kelsen, *Rapport sur la garantie juridictionnelle de la Constitution,* 94 ANNUAIRE DE L'INSTITUT INTERNATIONAL DE DROIT PUBLIC 127 (1929): "Cet effet *rétroactif* de l'annulation est une nécessité technique parce que, sans lui, les autorités chargées de l'application du droit n'auraient pas d'intérêt immédiat et par suite suffisamment puissant à provoquer l'intervention du tribunal constitutionnel. . . . Il faut les encourager à présenter ces requêtes en attribuant dans ce cas à l'annulation un effet rétroactif." *See also* GRANT, *supra* note 12, at 85 f.

[21] *See* Kauper, *supra* note 1, at 629 f.; GRANT, *supra* note 12, at 42 ff.; WAGNER, *supra* note 1, at 102 f., where there is a mention of the incisive *dictum* of the American Supreme Court (in Chicot County Drainage District v. Baxter State Bank, 308 U.S. 371, 374 (1940)): "The past cannot always be erased by a new judicial declaration. . . . These questions are among the most difficult of those which have engaged the attention of courts, state and

been the stimulation of those legal realists who have shown how the Constitution is a "living document" and subject to continuous evolution, so that a law, declared at one time to be unconstitutional, could at another time have been perfectly valid at that point of the Constitution's evolution.[22]

Thus buttressed, the American Supreme Court has in recent cases seemed to abandon explicit presumptions of either retroactivity or prospectivity and instead has balanced, case by case, questions of public policy and private rights. "Public policies" have been called by many names but nearly all have been used to support a denial of retroactivity by being lumped together under the two catch-words: "reliance" and "finality." The idea is that embodied in the old doctrine of res judicata: the need for certainty as to the law, for stable judgments upon which the population can gauge its actions, and for avoiding unnecessary conflict between the courts and the other branches of government, means that judi-

---

federal, and it is manifest from numerous decisions that an all-inclusive statement of a principle of absolute retroactive invalidity cannot be justified." For an excellent recent analysis of the retroactivity issue in the United States see Note, Retroactivity of Criminal Procedure Decisions, 55 IOWA L. REV. 1309 (1970). See also N.T. DOWLING & G. GUNTHER, CASES AND MATERIALS ON CONSTITUTIONAL LAW 30 ff., 892 ff. (Brooklyn, The Foundation Press, 8th ed. 1970). On the complex problem of the retroactivity of judgments in constitutional matters in American law, one might refer, for further information and references, to two recent comparative studies, both of considerable interest: W. KNITTEL, ZUM PROBLEM DER RÜCKWIRKUNG BEI EINER ÄNDERUNG DER RECHT-SPRECHUNG. EINE UNTERSUCHUNG ZUM DEUTSCHEN UND US-AMERIKANISCHEN RECHT (Bielefeld, Gieseking, 1965); Comoglio, Diritto di difesa e retroattività delle decisioni costituzionali, 22 RIVISTA DI DIRITTO PROCESSUALE 75 ff. (1967). The whole problem of retroactivity in the United States is, of course, intimately bound up with the American concept of judicial review: it is noteworthy that the decision in Linkletter v. Walker, 381 U.S. 618 (1965), begins by contrasting the philosophies of Blackstone (declaratory theory) and Austin (positivist): the Court itself seems to feel the need to fit the essentially political considerations behind a decision of retroactivity or prospectivity into a historical and judicial framework. Cf. Mishkin, supra note 6; Schwartz, Retroactivity, Reliability, and Due Process: A Reply to Professor Mishkin, 33 U. CHI. L. REV. 719-68 (1966); Note, supra at 1309 ff.

[22] A pragmatic approach is reflected also in Italy (see esp. art. 30, paras. 3 and 4 of the law of March 11, 1953, No. 87) and Germany (§ 79 of the Bundesverfassungsgerichtsgesetz of March 12, 1951). See, e.g., LECHNER, supra note 17, at 280 ff.; Friesenhahn, supra note 17, at 143; Geck, supra note 14, at 282 f., with a misunderstanding, however, as to the Italian solution. It now seems clear that the American Supreme Court would, in an appropriate situation, declare a purely prospective rule, not even applicable to the case before it. England v. Louisiana State Bd. of Medical Examiners, 375 U.S. 411, 422 (1964). See Note, supra note 21, at 1315 f. In previous cases the Supreme Court upheld such a practice by state courts, Great Northern Ry. v. Sunburst Oil & Ref. Co., 287 U.S. 358 (1932), while avoiding the practice itself. See generally H.M. HART & A. SACKS, THE LEGAL PROCESS: BASIC PROBLEMS IN THE MAKING AND APPLICATION OF LAW 620-37 (Cambridge, tentative ed. 1958).

cial decisions which have become final and are beyond direct attack are "vested" and should not be upset save for the most
pressing reasons.[23] A similar philosophy prevails in Italy and Germany, where the tendency has been to respect certain "consolidated
effects," due to acts based on laws later declared contrary to the
constitution.[24]

c) *The criminal defendant:* In both systems of review there is
one case which argues most strongly for the retroactive application
of a constitutional decision. It is that of the person who is serving
a criminal sentence after being convicted of violating a law subsequently declared unconstitutional. Italy and Germany, by statute,
and the United States, by case law, have all looked favorably on
petitions for release in such cases.[25]

But what of the prisoner whose *crime* remains on the books,
but whose conviction was brought about through *procedures* subsequently found to violate his basic rights (to an attorney, to im-
munity from arbitrary searches, against self-incrimination, etc.)?
The conviction may be "final," but the execution of the sentence
continues; nor, with the availability of remedies like habeas corpus,

---

[23] *Cf.* Cleary, *Res Judicata Reexamined,* 57 YALE L.J. 339 ff. (1948).

[24] *See* Engelhardt, *supra* note 17, at 134 f.; Sandulli, *Natura, funzione ed
effetti delle pronunce della Corte costituzionale sulla legittimità delle leggi,* 9
RIVISTA TRIMESTRALE DI DIRITTO PUBBLICO 23, 39 (1959).
The topic of the effects of judgments on the constitutionality of laws brings
with it a host of complex problems, both theoretical and practical, many of
which one cannot even mention in these pages. For example, there is the problem of which law is applicable in place of the one declared unconstitutional
(*see* Engelhardt, *supra* at 134); the problem of the effect of a judgment up-
holding the constitutionality of a law (*see, e.g.,* Cappelletti, *Pronunce di
rigetto nel processo costituzionale delle libertà e cosa giudicata,* 11 (pt. 1)
RIVISTA DI DIRITTO PROCESSUALE 135 ff. (1956)); the problem of the effect of
the reasons given for constitutional decisions, for instance when a law is upheld by the Constitutional Court due to a certain interpretation (*see* Engelhardt, *supra* at 137 f.; Cappelletti, *Sentenze condizionali della Corte costituzionale,* 12 RIVISTA DI DIRITTO PROCESSUALE 88 ff. (1957)); the problem of
the retroactivity of a judgment contrary to previous decisions (*see* KNITTEL,
supra note 21); and so on. On the whole, these problems are treated with
such variations from country to country, that it would be impossible to give
a useful synthesis in comparative terms.

[25] In criminal, as well as civil cases, Austria still stands by the strict
rule of nonretroactivity, save as regards the parties to the case in which the
law is found unconstitutional. Perhaps it is in the Austrian criminal case that
one sees most clearly the competition between values which characterizes all
decisions regarding retroactivity. On the one hand, there is the argument for
"equal protection" for all persons convicted under the same criminal statute
("it does not seem that the mere time factor, the somewhat accidental moment of the judgment, should thus determine rights and duties"). On the other,
there is the Austrian emphasis on the "stability of the legal order and the
faith people place in it." Geck, *supra* note 14, at 283 f. It hardly seems, however, that "legal stability" is sufficient justification for the continued imprison-
ment of a person convicted under an unconstitutional statute.

can it be said that the proceeding is immune from judicial attack.[26] Yet the spectre of thousands of prisoners, convicted under old procedures, asking for their liberty, is one which haunts, perhaps needlessly, law enforcement officials and public alike. The debate continues on both sides of the Atlantic, the courts in the United States, for example, favoring individual petitioners only when the procedural right denied affected the reliability of the earlier fact-finding process.[27]

---

[26] Germany has by specific statutory provision extended an already existing statutory device to allow a prisoner to reopen his trial *(Wiederaufnahme)*, though his conviction may have long before become "final," if the statute under which he was convicted is later declared unconstitutional. See § 79(1) of the *Bundesverfassungsgerichtsgesetz*. Whether one can avail himself of the *Wiederaufnahme* if the *procedures* used to convict are later declared unconstitutional, is a question which has been debated by legal scholars but which has been decided negatively by the Federal Constitutional Court. See the decision of July 7, 1960, 11 ENTSCHEIDUNGEN DES BUNDESVERFASSUNGSGE-RICHTS 263 ff. (1961), and references in LECHNER, *supra* note 17 at 281; BÖCKENFÖRDE, *supra* note 17, at 70 ff., 91 ff.

Italy presents a similar situation. Art. 30, para. 4, of the law of March 11, 1953, No. 87, on the Constitutional Court provides that the execution of a criminal judgment, though final, based on a law later held to be unconstitutional, ceases immediately upon the declaration of unconstitutionality. This provision has been interpreted as applying only to substantive law. *See, e.g.,* the decision of the Constitutional Court of December 29, 1966, No. 127, 11 GIURISPRUDENZA COSTITUZIONALE 1697 ff. (1966). This restrictive interpretation has been criticized in M. CAPPELLETTI, PROCESSO E IDEOLOGIE 256 f. (Bologna, Il Mulino, 1969); Comoglio, *supra* note 21, at 93; Vigoriti, *Problemi del processo costituzionale: poteri discrezionali dei giudici ed efficacia nel tempo della sentenza,* 20 RIVISTA TRIMESTRALE DI DIRITTO E PROCEDURA CIVILE 1474, 1493 (1967).

[27] The "reliability" test is far from perfect since many of the "new" constitutional, procedural rights of defendants are meant to protect *both* the dignity of the accused as well as the integrity of the fact finding process. It may be clear that denial of an attorney to an indigent probably prevents an adequate presentation of all relevant facts to the court, and that the guarantee of legal counsel for such defendants should be applied retroactively. It may also be obvious that some illegally obtained evidence retains its probative value and that the decision to exclude such evidence might best be applied prospectively only. Other situations are less clear: a prosecutor who "disinterestedly" informs the jury that the accused has refused to testify certainly affects the ability of the jury to decide the case objectively. Yet the banning of this practice by the Supreme Court was not applied retroactively (Tehan v. United States *ex rel.* Shott, 382 U.S. 406 (1966)). Double jeopardy and cruel and unusual punishments, if inflicted on a defendant, have little to do with "fact finding," but have a great deal to do with human dignity, so much so that a refusal to give relief retroactively to the prisoner serving a "cruel" sentence, or to the prisoner who was subjected to double jeopardy, would seem shocking indeed. *See* Schwartz, *supra* note 21, at 724 ff., 741.

Perhaps realizing these shortcomings, many of the recent decisions of the Supreme Court while denying *general* retroactive effect to certain procedural guarantees, have affirmed the right of a prisoner convicted under subsequently invalidated procedures to bring a writ of habeas corpus based on a claim of special prejudice in his own case, caused by the denial of any procedural right. *See* Linkletter v. Walker, 381 U.S. 618 (1965); Johnson v. New Jersey, 384 U.S. 719 (1966).

CONCLUSION

Judicial review is a theme with many variations and subtle implications. The basic *motif* is a product of our common western history; the variations arise inevitably from differences of experience and outlook within this larger framework. The subtleties, finally, center about the ambiguous nature of judicial review in any democratic state.

The theme of modern constitutionalism is the embodiment of "natural law" principles in the positive law of the state. While classical antiquity and medieval Europe had at times affirmed the theoretical right of the citizen to disobey the unjust law, the right remained theory only. It was left to times nearer our own to seek an instrument to protect principles considered fundamental.

With the French Revolution there was a temporary split in the evolutionary pattern of the West. The newly freed American colonies clung to older concepts which subordinated both the executive and the legislature to a higher law, and gave new meaning to these ideas by embodying the higher law in a written Constitution interpreted and applied by the judges. Continental Europe, however, chose to move from concepts of "natural justice" toward those of "legal justice."[1] The popular legislature was seen as the best guarantor of universal values. It was given the duty of codifying the law, and institutions like *Cassation* were meant to ensure the conformity of other state action to the standards of the codes.

After the sad experiences of the first half of this century, there arose in Europe the need to put a check upon the legislature itself, for it had become evident that even legislation could be the source of great abuses such as the racial persecutions, which were authorized by statute. Hence Europeans, and non-Europeans as well, embarked on the path taken by the Americans so long before. "Higher law" was to be expressed in constitutions that were difficult to amend; the judiciary, or a part of it, was to be the instrument for assuring conformity to this higher law. The Old World moved from "legal" to "constitutional justice."[2]

---

[1] See Ch. II, § 6 *supra*.
[2] See Ch. II *supra*.

Though civil and common law countries are back on the same road, differences in approach to judicial review remain as a testimony to past divergences. The United States, and those countries which have followed its example, strive to this day to confine judicial review within the traditional *judicial* framework, the political nature of the institution being, whenever possible, carefully disguised. The civil law countries, with specially appointed courts, utilize special procedures to focus directly on statutes, not cases, and thus take a franker view of the whole process. Yet, paradoxically, the elaborate fictions of the American judges may well allow them to perform their *political* functions less dangerously than do their European brethren.[3]

So it is that in spite of its nearly universal appeal, judicial review remains an enigmatic institution. It operates principally in states with democratic philosophies; yet it claims the right to frustrate, in certain situations, the will of the majority.[4] Its decisions are often pre-eminently political, yet they are made by men not themselves responsible to the electorate. The theoretical power of the judge of constitutionality is awesome; yet in the end he has "neither sword nor purse" and must depend on others to give his decision meaning.

Much that is relevant to this we have left unsaid—or incompletely said. There is, for example, the creative element of interpretation. When a judge interprets a statute in order to avoid a constitutional question, or when he redraws a law, omitting the parts he considers unconstitutional, he is, in a sense, legislating. For Americans this raises questions of the validity of the old declaratory theory of the courts' function and of Marshall's time-hallowed reasoning. For many Europeans the very assumption of an interpretative power by a constitutional court is a violation of the mandate which reserved such powers to the highest ordinary courts.[5]

Also noteworthy is the form taken by decisions of most of the special constitutional courts, whose judges do not have the right to publish dissenting or concurring opinions. In striving for outward uniformity, it seems that the centralized systems may sacri-

---

[3] See Chs. III and IV, and especially Ch. IV, § 6 *supra.*

[4] *Cf., e.g.,* H.E. DEAN, JUDICIAL REVIEW AND DEMOCRACY (New York, Random House, 1966); E.V. ROSTOW, *The Democratic Character of Judicial Review,* in THE SOVEREIGN PREROGATIVE. THE SUPREME COURT AND THE QUEST FOR LAW 147-92 (New Haven, Yale University Press, 1962).

[5] On the declaratory theory and Marshall's reasoning see Ch. II, §§ 1, 5, Ch. III, § 3 and Ch. V, § 3 *supra;* on the right of the special constitutional courts to interpret statutes see Ch. IV, notes 29-30, and Ch. V, note 8 *supra.*

fice the wealth of nuance which often characterizes decisions by the United States Supreme Court. This is, however, an area where radical changes are in progress.[6]

There is, moreover, the importance of procedure. Judicial review is but an empty promise if one can vindicate his rights only through long and expensive proceedings.[7] Yet bypassing traditional concepts of contentious review may give constitutional cases a non-adversary, "test case" character, with all the consequent implications for *res judicata* and advisory opinion concepts.

Nor has anything been said of the difference between "formal" and "material" conformity to a constitution. Yet some countries which refuse their courts the right to inquire into the agreement of a statute with the substantive content of the constitution may well permit the judges to ask if the law was passed and promulgated in accord with the procedures prescribed by that document.[8]

---

[6] For examples of the movement in favor of publishing the dissenting opinions of the judges of the special constitutional courts see: M. CAPPELLETTI, PROCESSO E IDEOLOGIE 28 f. (Bologna, Il Mulino, 1969); W. HEYDE, DAS MINDERHEITSVOTUM DES ÜBERSTIMMTEN RICHTERS (Bielefeld, Gieseking, 1966); E. McWHINNEY, JUDICIAL REVIEW 225 ff. (University of Toronto Press, 4th ed. 1969); LE OPINIONI DISSENZIENTI DEI GIUDICI COSTITUZIONALI ED INTERNAZIONALI (C. Mortati (ed.), Milano, Giuffrè, 1964); Arndt, *Nachlese zur dissenting opinion*, in 1 JUS PRIVATUM GENTIUM. FESTSCHRIFT FÜR MAX RHEINSTEIN ZUM 70. GEBURTSTAG AM 5. JULI 1969, at 127-46 (Tübingen, Mohr, 1969); Friesenhahn, *Die Verfassungsgerichtsbarkeit in der Bundesrepublik Deutchland*, in MAX-PLANCK-INSTITUT FÜR AUSLÄNDISCHES ÖFFENTLICHES RECHT UND VÖLKERRECHT, VERFASSUNGSGERICHTSBARKEIT IN DER GEGENWART. LÄNDERBERICHTE UND RECHTSVERGLEICHUNG 188 f. (H. Mosler (ed.), Köln-Berlin, Heymanns, 1962); Rupp, *Zur Frage der Dissenting Opinion*, in 2 DIE MODERNE DEMOKRATIE UND IHR RECHT. FESTSCHRIFT FÜR GERHARD LEIBHOLZ ZUM 65. GEBURTSTAG 531 ff. (Tübingen, Mohr, 1966); Zweigert, *Empfiehlt es sich, die Bekanntgabe der abweichenden Meinung des überstimmten Richters (Dissenting Opinion) in den deutschen Verfahrensordnungen zuzulassen?*, in 1 VERHANDLUNGEN DES SIEBENUNDVIERZIGSTEN DEUTSCHEN JURISTENTAGES-NÜRNBERG 1968 (München, Beck, 1968); Berger, *Empfiehlt sich die Bekanntgabe abweichender Meinungen überstimmter Richter?*, 21 NEUE JURISTISCHE WOCHENSCHRIFT 961 ff. (1968); Cappelletti, *Ideologie nel diritto processuale*, 16 RIVISTA TRIMESTRALE DI DIRITTO E PROCEDURA CIVILE 214 f. (1962); Cole, *Three Constitutional Courts: A Comparison*, 53 AM. POL. SCI. REV. 963, 969 (1959); Federer, *Die Bekanntgabe der abweichenden Meinung des überstimmten Richters*, 23 JURISTENZEITUNG 511 ff. (1968); Nadelmann, *Non-Disclosure of Dissents in Constitutional Courts: Italy and West Germany*, 13 AM. J. COMP. L. 268 ff. (1964).

The positive results of this movement may be seen in Germany where a recent statute allows individual judges of the Constitutional Court to publish dissenting and concurring opinions. Law of Dec. 21, 1970, in BUNDESGESETZBLATT part I, of Dec. 24, 1970.

In Italy art. 5, para. 2 of the *Regolamento generale* of the Constitutional Court (GAZZETTA UFFICIALE, Feb. 19, 1966, special issue) allows minority judges to record the fact of their dissent which, however, remains an internal document of the Court and is not published.

[7] Ch. IV, § 5 *supra*.

[8] Italy, under the Albertine statute, allowed such a control of "formal"

Yet, beyond these issues, what is most important is the break-down of the old dichotomies. There was, perhaps, too much emphasis on *difference* when such distinctions were made as those between "natural" and "positive" law, "centralized" and "decentralized" review, control *incidenter* and *principaliter*, *erga omnes* and *inter partes* decisions, retroactive and prospective effects, as well as between the "civil law" and "common law" worlds. The two worlds are becoming one, certainly in terms of the questions that have been discussed in this study. On both sides of the Atlantic, constitutional lawyers talk of the dangers, or advantages, of judicial activism, of the creative aspect of judicial interpretation, of the rights of the accused, and so on. Insofar as judicial review has encouraged this convergence, it has further justified itself.

---

constitutionality. *See* C. Esposito, La validità delle leggi (Milano, Giuffrè, 2d ed. 1964).

It may also be true that France, though not allowing genuine judicial review, may yet permit a formal control of legislation by the courts in the course of concrete cases. Although French judges are forbidden to judge upon the material constitutionality of legislation they "do not reject the idea of controlling the 'formal' or 'extrinsic' unconstitutionality of enactments published as 'laws,' that is to ascertain whether the supposed law has been passed according to the constitutional rules on legislative procedure and regularly promulgated." Eisenmann & Hamon, *La Juridiction Constitutionnelle en Droit Français*, in Max-Planck-Institut, *supra* note 6, at 241. On the specific point of "formal" and "material" review in Norway, Denmark and Switzerland, see Castberg, *Verfassungsgerichtsbarkeit in Norwegen und Dänemark*, in *id.* at 426-28; Imboden, *Verfassungsgerichtsbarkeit in der Schweiz*, in *id.* at 514 f. *See also* Geck, *Judicial Review of Statutes: A Comparative Survey of Present Institutions and Practices*, 51 Cornell L.Q. 250, 255 (1966).

TABLE OF CASES

SUBJECT INDEX

DATE DUE

11. 05. '81	
11. 05. '81	
JUN 19 '91	
OCT 1 1 1999	

BRODART, INC.   Cat. No. 23-221